Short Back and Sides

Short Back and Sides

Tales from an Irish Barber Shop

Peter Quinn

Gill & Macmillan

Gill & Macmillan
Hume Avenue, Park West, Dublin 12
with associated companies throughout the world
www.gillmacmillan.ie

© Peter Quinn 2011
978 07171 4941 4

Illustrations by Eoin Coveney
Typography design and print origination by TypeIT, Dublin
Printed in the UK by CPI Cox & Wyman, Reading

This book is typeset in 11.5 Bembo on 13.

The paper used in this book comes from the wood pulp of managed forests.
For every tree felled, at least one tree is planted, thereby renewing natural
resources.

A CIP catalogue record for this book is available from the British Library.

5 4 3 2 1

Barber-shop conversations

I consider myself lucky to be doing something I enjoy for a living at a time when having work of any description is a privilege. It's something I'm reminded of regularly by customers who have lost their job over the last couple of years since the 'Celtic Tiger' collapsed and died, leaving us to foot the bill for his extravagant lifestyle. But, recession or not, hair continues to grow, barbers keep cutting and where there are people there is conversation.

There's something about barber-shop conversations that sets them apart from the usual small talk that's normal in a business environment, and in fact these exchanges are enjoyed on both sides of the chair. There are of course people who don't want conversation to be part of the service, and there are a few shops that offer haircuts without the traditional banter; but, for the majority of barber-shop customers, the chat seals the deal, and some regulars who wait for a specific barber will tell you that it's 'for the chat rather than the haircut.' I like to think it's both, but as long as they keep coming I can't complain!

The most popular subject of conversation in Ireland is the weather, so it should be no surprise that it's top of the list in the barber shop. But, as a customer once remarked, 'It breaks the ice!' From day to day, leaving the weather aside, customers talk mainly about the current news stories, which can include world events, politics (quite a hot subject at the moment), the recession and, of course, the banks. Funny stories will always be a part of a working day down at the shop, but they're not as plentiful as they used to be.

Over the last few years there has been a shift in the mood, and the stories we hear are more weighty than ever before. Fortunes were made and lost in recent years, debts and negative equity are a part of everyday life and, as always in a time of economic depression, there are those who have to leave the country for work. The stories these customers tell range from funny to eye-opening, but all are interesting in their openness, and they paint a picture of the difficulties some people have faced in recent years. Despite the extremes in the weather and the economy, the fall of the church and the spiralling cost of the bank bail-out, there is plenty of upbeat talk, and some people even make light of their problems.

After these most popular subjects, the remaining conversations can be about anything and everything, from the sublime to the surreal, and as individual as the customer and their hairstyle. The view from the barber's chair gives the impression that we're a nation of optimists: the way we all look forward to the summer every year is proof enough. Either that or we're in denial—and I don't mean the river in Egypt!

Listening to customers, we (the barbers) are informed of what's happening in the world outside, keeping us on the cutting edge with the low-down on what's up. Information that falls through the cracks of the mainstream media is discussed, conspiracy theories are debated and there are opinions on everything from global warming to religion. We hear about the best and the worst of everything: no-one talks about films, restaurants, books, albums or concerts that are just 'okay'. They recommend the best—and the worst makes for a good story. We hear about far-off places: the popular and the areas less travelled. The descriptions are sometimes so vivid that I often feel like I've been there myself.

Now and again we hear a story that will become a news item a few weeks or months later. I've often been amazed at what people will tell us while they're in the chair. I suppose they're just getting it off their chest—lightening the load, so to speak. I remember a famous court case, and one of the jurors was getting his hair cut. The conversation started with 'I'm not allowed to talk about the trial, but . . .' and he began to tell me everything that happened that morning in the courtroom! I can't remember a time when there was so much being discussed in the barber shop—it's really unprecedented. Customers are genuinely concerned about the future and are even more concerned about who might lead us out of the mess we're in.

For some reason, a lot of the stories I heard would keep coming back to me—not just the funny stories but the serious ones too. I thought it would be an idea to start writing them down. I had played with the idea of trying to get a regular newspaper article and, after talking to journalists who liked the idea, I kept at it. I felt like I was on to something, but I didn't know what just yet. I also thought it would be a way of clearing the stories out of my head. Eventually I had enough material to fill a book, and I decided to go to a publisher, leaving the newspaper column idea in the wake, and that's how this book came to be. Almost every day, while I'm mining away at the coal face, there will be a jewel that stands out during a conversation, and I write it down. So, keeping that in mind, it's the customers who are the real stars of this book. It's their comments, witty remarks and stories that have kept me amused and engaged all these years I've been cutting their hair.

I've dated the entries like a diary or a blog, which is useful for noting when events occurred. The dates are never exact, as I hear the stories after the event has happened, so they're only a rough guide. I can't be held responsible for what's said or how much is true—that's for you to decide. I'm just recording what I hear. In some cases the stories may be hard to believe, but truth, as we know, can sometimes be stranger than fiction. (The story of Paddy Hitler is a good example. It's true, by the way—I checked it out.)

So, if you're feeling like you need a lift, go down to your local barber shop and, as a customer from Cork once put it, 'It always puts a spring in my step when I get a haircut!' Or you could read a book of barber-shop conversations!

Don't forget you can post your own barber-shop stories at www.facebook.com/shortbackandsidesbook.

Aurora borealis on tour

Ireland, believe it or not, January 2005

Customer: I saw the aurora borealis the other night!

Barber: There was a great picture on the front of the *Irish Times* yesterday with the lights in the sky over Benbulbin in Sligo.

Customer: Well, I was watching the news on TV3, and they said it would be visible over Dublin if you went up the mountains away from the light pollution, so I went up. It really was something to see. It was like rolling clouds of green and red in the sky.

Barber: I'd love to have seen that. Was there many up there?

Customer: There were about 150—maybe more! People were spread out along the Feather Bed—hard to guess. A lad near me made a call on his mobile, and all I could hear was 'Jimmy, get the chip-van up here quick!'

The Passion of the Christ

2 February 2005

Barber: Have you see that new Mel Gibson movie?

Customer: *The Passion of the Christ*? No, not yet.

Barber: I hear it's based on a true story.

UFO

4 February 2007. Before the first rugby game played in Croke Park.

Customer: There's a great picture in the paper of the UFO over Croke Park.

Barber: A UFO?

Customer: Yeah, it's there, look [showing me the picture], above the stadium. It's a rugby ball!

History in the making (the good old days)

2 April 2007

Customer: Can you believe the times we're living in? It's really something! Like the picture in the papers recently on the front page of Gerry Adams and Ian Paisley agreeing to share power in the North. The Irish cricket team, who no-one's ever heard of, beat Pakistan on Paddy's Day, and the rugby team thrashed England in Croke Park! History is being made.

Barber: Anything is possible in this country right now. The economy is booming—this is as good as it gets. The pigs will be flying next!

Customer (sitting in the next chair listening): They are already, you know. They have helicopters now!

The Irish cricket team

6 April 2007

Customer: We were away in New York when the Irish cricket team beat Pakistan. We didn't know about it at the time, but we got into a cab with a Pakistani driver who got a bit hyper when we told him we were Irish. He told us that Pakistan had just lost to Ireland in the cricket, and we started laughing and asked him if he was sure it was Ireland they were beaten by, which made him even more agitated. He pulled in to the side of the road and threw us out of his cab!

Barber: That's a bit of an over-reaction.

Customer: True. We were thinking afterwards he must have been pissed that not only were they—the great Pakistan—beaten by a much less experienced team—you know, us—against all the odds; but, to add insult to injury, we didn't even know there was an Irish cricket team!

Noah's ark

24 June 2007

Barber: You're next there.

Customer (after sitting into the chair): Just a general trim.

Barber: Okay, sir.

Customer: Terrible weather, isn't it? Never seen the like of it: constant rain, constant rain—it's been raining for forty-eight days consecutively.

Barber: It's all that Rihanna's fault. Since her song 'Umbrella' topped the charts at the end of May the rain hasn't stopped. In fact, some of the radio stations are putting a ban on the song!

Customer (being very serious): It's bad, all right. Never heard of Rihanna, but, you know, I heard that there's a lad in Wicklow building an ark!

4

Turn down that racket!

11 October 2007

At Croke Park the Police played a sell-out concert. It turned out, as I heard from many people who were there, to be a disappointment. A customer whose hair I was cutting told me he left the concert to go to the bar in the stadium. Remember, fans had paid good money for those tickets.

Customer: I went to the Police concert on Saturday.

Barber: Was it good?

Customer: It wasn't great, but the Rugby World Cup quarter-final was on, so I headed up to the bar to watch it. When I got there I couldn't believe how packed it was. Obviously I wasn't the only one who decided to watch the game instead. I was half in and half out, and as a result the door couldn't close behind me. The concert was in full swing, and, as I waited there for an opportunity to step in, a voice shouted out, 'Shut that door. We can't hear the bleedin' match!'

Obama

8 November 2008

Customer: They've got a black lad in the White House!

On Bush

10 November 2008

Customer: Bush was such a bad president they say it will be difficult for a white man to ever get elected again!

A Taoiseach's salary

16 November 2008

Customer: Did you see what our ministers and Taoiseach earn? My God, Bertie earns more than Obama!

Barber: We should write Obama a letter offering him the job here—a heartfelt letter from the Irish people. And, seeing that he has relations here, and the bigger salary, he just might go for it!

Customer: Worth a try!

Après match

2 February 2009

Customer: A friend of mine is a guard in a small town in the country, and he was working at a checkpoint, stopping people and breathalysing them. It was early in the days of the drink-and-drive crackdown, and in the country some people were slow to change their ways.

There had been an all-Ireland final on that day, and the county had won. I can't say any names or give too much detail, but one of the players—who's well known—was stopped at the checkpoint. My friend (the guard) congratulated him on the win. 'Jaysus, we did it. Still can't believe it!' said the player. 'Were you drinking?' asked the guard. 'I was, of course,' says the player. 'Sure it's a day to celebrate! I had about fifteen pints and God knows how many shots!' 'I'm afraid I'll have to breathalyse you,' says the guard. The player gives the guard a confused look. 'Why?' he says. 'Do you not believe me?'

Arctic diversion

17 February 2009

Customer: Did you hear they diverted all the flights from the Arctic?

Barber: No, why have they done that?

Customer: Well, when a plane flew over, the penguins would hear the noise, you see, and they all looked up. And, as they can only look so far as the plane went over, they'd be staring at it, and suddenly they'd all fall over backwards like dominoes! Trouble was, they couldn't get back up on their feet after. So many of them were dying they had to divert the flights.

Clever entrepreneurs

2 March 2009

Customer: Because of the recession, developers who have large amounts of unsold apartments found would-be buyers walking away after seeing no-one was living there.

Barber: I've seen lots of empty apartments around, and I was wondering how they could be sold. No-one wants to be in a ghost development!

Customer: That's exactly it. The new entrepreneurial idea was to sell patio furniture, potted plants and second-hand bicycles to these developers to put on the empty unfurnished balconies and make the apartments look—from the outside at least—as though they were lived in. You have been warned!

Trolley dollies
9 March 2009

Barber: How are things in the restaurant business these days?

Customer: They were bad for a few months, but it's getting better. We had a brainstorming session and came up with a few ideas.

Barber: Everyone is looking for ideas to get business going. What did you do?

Customer: Well, the one that worked best was to get the desserts selling. Since the recession they haven't been selling at all, so we hired a dolly bird, and she pushes a trolley of desserts around the restaurant. Businessmen who come in for lunch call her over to talk to her, and they buy a dessert.

Barber: A trolley dolly! That's sexist but brilliant!

Customer: What can I say—it works!

The jingle post
3 April 2009

Customer: Have you heard about the jingle post?

Barber: No, what is it?

Customer: The jingle post is what the banks across the country call the letters in the morning post that make a jingling sound. It's the sound of house and apartment keys being returned by home-owners who've decided, for their own reasons, to opt out of the deal. It's become such a regular occurrence that it's earned the name 'the jingle post'!

Barber: Dark days indeed.

Recycling tip for junk mail!

5 April 2009

Customer: I thought of a great way to get rid of junk mail.

Barber: I'm getting a serious amount of it. My neighbour has taped up her letterbox.

Customer: Well, you just keep all the junk mail, and when your Visa bill arrives you'll find a freepost envelope in there, so you take the freepost envelope and put all your junk mail into it and post it off to Visa!

Barber: I'm sure if this catches on there won't be a freepost envelope in future!

Not so loud

6 April 2009

Customer: Can I get a Portuguese mullet?

That's the code for 'Ronaldo-style' for customers who are embarrassed to say Ronaldo out loud in front of the queue.

Alopecia

7 April 2009

Customer: How's my hair looking there?

Barber: You have alopecia [hair falling out]. Have you seen a doctor about it?

Customer: Yeah, I got a prescription for it. He says it's caused by stress.

Barber: That's right. Have you had anything unusually stressful going on recently?

Customer: Yeah, I'm a bit stressed about losing my feckin' hair!

Culture shock
9 April 2009

Barber 1 (from Iraq): Is it against the law to beat your wife in Ireland?

Barber 2 (and some customers): Yes, of course it is!

Barber 1: Oh.

He just went back to cutting his customer's hair. Priceless!

Jet lag
11 April 2009

Customer (a barman from Temple Bar): I had a crowd of English lads in a few weeks ago, and they were asking me what the time difference was.

Barber: What did they mean?

Customer: Well, it turns out they wanted to know what the time difference between England and Ireland was, because they saw a clock on O'Connell Street that was an hour behind! What do they teach those lads in school?

Barber: They never seem to put the clocks back in town when the hour changes, so for six months they're an hour behind!

Che Shay

12 April 2009

Talking to a customer about the film *Che*, the biopic about Che Guevara.

Customer: Che Guevara was of Irish descent. His mother was Irish. Did you know?

Barber: There are Irish everywhere, but I never heard that.

Customer: They only called him Che like a nickname. Sure wasn't he christened Seamus!

Barber: Seamus Guevara—I like it.

Atten?

14 April 2009

A woman who worked in the shop with us for a few years was always going on holidays. She did this so often that I used to tell customers that she was moonlighting as a flight attendant. One day a customer asked where she was, while getting his hair cut . . .

Customer: So where's Sheila today?

Barber: Oh, she's in at ten.

Customer: Atten? Where's that?

Barber: No, no, she's not in until ten!

Yoko

16 April 2009

A customer I knew well was in for a haircut, and during the conversation I asked him where a mutual friend had been, as I hadn't seen him for a long time.

Both of the lads were in a band together for many years, and I'd been cutting their hair for a long time.

Barber: So where's Alan these days? It's been a while since he's been in.

Customer: I haven't seen him for a few weeks either. He's got a new girlfriend. Seems serious too. We call her Yoko.

Barber: Yoko? Why do you call her Yoko?

Customer: She broke up the band.

Financial crisis

18 April 2009

After the bank crash in September 2008 a customer remarked wittily: 'When the tide goes out you can see whose trousers are down.'

At the races

19 April 2009

Customer: A group of builders and developers who were at the Galway Races were overheard playing 'Who Used to Be a Millionaire?'

More financial crisis remarks

20 April 2009

A customer told me during a chat about the state of all things financial that 'unfortunately, most of the builders and bankers weren't in the tomorrow business.'

Fake tan
21 April 2009

I had a Spanish student in for a haircut recently. He'd only been here a few days. When we were talking about his initial impressions of Ireland he asked me why so many of the women have orange skin!

Bank policy
22 April 2009

Customer: The banks will give you an umbrella when the weather is good and take it back when it rains!

Exam weather
23 April 2009

Customer: Well, it's that time of year again, and as usual the weather is great! How is it that every year the sun comes out just before the Junior Cert and Leaving?

Barber: You could put money on the sun coming out this time every year!

Customer: Enjoy it while it lasts. I'm off to get some stuff for the barbecue before it's all sold out. See you in a few weeks!

Courtmacsherry
24 April 2009

A customer who was on holiday in Co. Cork was given a bumper sticker to advertise the area where he was staying. It read 'Courtmacsherry—a quiet drinking village with a fishing problem.'

The sweetest revenge

26 April 2009

There are times in the barber shop when someone will impart a pearl of wisdom born of their life's experience. One customer told me in no uncertain terms that 'if another man ever tries to run away with your wife or girlfriend the best revenge you can get is to let him.'

Iraqi weather

27 April 2009

It was raining again, but as usual there were moments of sunshine in between.

Customer: When will this Iraqi weather ever end!

Barber: Iraqi weather? What do you mean?

Customer: It's the same day in and day out: Sunni and Shi'ite!

You don't know what a recession is!

28 April 2009

Young customer (a student): This recession is terrible. We can't get away to work for the summer because there are no jobs anywhere, and I haven't the money to go out and get smashed at the weekend. The summer is going to be tough. At least I'm not finished college this year.

Barber: Yeah, it's affecting everyone. It's all I hear lately: recession, recession, recession . . .

Older customer (in the next chair): You don't know what you're talking about. You haven't lived through a recession. This is a privileged recession. You have so much compared with what it was like in the past, and no-one will go hungry. When I was young I had one pair of jeans, and I had to stay in on a Sunday morning while my mother washed them!

Everyone just burst out laughing.

How to catch a cold

29 April 2009

A customer was sniffling while I was cutting his hair. I brought him a box of tissues and left them beside him. The customer in the next chair having his hair done noticed and was watching.

Barber: I see you have a touch of a cold there.

Customer 1: Yes, I was out for a few drinks last night, and I woke up sneezing this morning.

Customer 2 (in the next chair): Well, that's what you get for drinking out of a damp glass!

Frustrated tourist

30 April 2009

Customer (on holiday from America): Went down to Croke Park with the kids the other day, and it was gone!

Barber: Gone? What do you mean, gone?

Customer: There's no park there: they've built a stadium on it.

Male chauvinist
1 May 2009

Customer: Do you know that there's only one thing worse than a male chauvinist pig?

Barber: And what's that?

Customer: A woman who won't do what she's told!

The mysterious case of the missing gnome
2 May 2009

There was a peculiar house in Rathfarnham, Co. Dublin, which was brightly painted and had, I think, salmon-coloured roof tiles. I heard many stories about that house—even that it had been sponsored by Dulux! It was known to many people for the number of gnomes in the front garden—there must have been fifty or more. One day while I was working away a customer told me about the house. I had seen it once or twice, so I knew it existed.

Customer: Did you hear about the gnome house?

Barber: No, what about it?

Customer: Well, two sisters live there. They're very proud of their gnomes, and they'd notice if one was missing, you see?

Barber: Okay.

Customer: Well, a few months ago, one of the gnomes disappeared! There was no sign of it anywhere, and the sisters thought maybe whoever took it would put it back. But weeks went by, and still no sign. Then, out of the blue, one morning they received a letter from

Australia. They opened it, and it was a letter from the gnome telling them not to worry, that he was fine, just wanted a bit of a holiday, and he was enjoying Sydney and hoping they weren't missing him too much. Also with the letter was a photo of the gnome, with Sydney Opera House in the background!

A little while later another letter arrived, and then another, each containing a photo of the gnome in various well-known exotic locations. Well, the sisters didn't know what it was at first, but after a while it seems to have been students travelling who took the gnome with them and who for a laugh were sending the photos and letters back.

Anyway, the summer's over now, and guess what: just the other morning the gnome was back in the garden!

Barber: Back from his travels!

This story later went out on the 'Gerry Ryan Show', and later a similar one appeared in 'Coronation Street'.

Next, please

3 May 2009

Customer: I need my hair cut badly.

Barber: No problem, sir, I can cut it badly for you.

Bail-out

4 May 2009

Customer: It's nearly eight months since the Government bail-out. You know, I had a suitcase packed and a flight booked to get out of here that night, only I waited. And I wasn't the only one—a lot of people in finance were ready to run!

Barber: We almost had a total meltdown. So how come you waited?

Customer: I was pacing the floor when my wife suggested I try to get some sleep and wait for the news that morning. I turned on the radio first thing, and it was announced in the headlines on 'Morning Ireland' that the Government was going to bail out the banks, and I couldn't believe my ears!

Barber: A close call!

Karma man

5 May 2009

A customer who was visiting India got a taxi from the airport to the hotel where he was staying. The driver was friendly and spoke English.

Customer: On the way to the hotel I told the driver to blow the horn at a car that made a dangerous swerve in front of us. 'Oh, no, I can't do that,' he said. 'Then someone will do it to me.' I thought he was just fobbing me off, but as we drove on I noticed in the mayhem that is normal driving on the streets in India that no-one blew their horn, no-one flashed their lights in anger and no-one rolled their window down and shouted abuse at careless drivers who caused them to brake hard. In fact, it was the opposite: everywhere I looked I saw genuine smiling faces behind windscreens or on bicycles. It was a real culture shock. 'It's karma,' the taxi-driver explained. 'Have you heard of it?' 'Yes,' I said, 'we call it "what goes around comes around".'

Television licence crackdown

6 May 2009

Back in the eighties there was a television licence crackdown, as I'd imagine that there were very few licence-holders in those dark days in Ireland.

Customer: I remember the TV licence inspectors had a white van with a radar-like attachment on the top of the roof that would drive around estates all through the summer months—back when we had real summers— and they were supposed to detect if you had a TV on in the house. The idea was that, if you had, they'd call to your door and ask to see your licence. It became known to everyone quite quickly, and the children playing outside would come running back to the house to tell you, and you'd switch the TV off until the van was gone. I remember a neighbour saying that when the children all came running you didn't know if it was the ice-cream van or the TV licence men!

Barber: I do remember hearing something like that before. It's so funny. Imagine the boardroom meeting—coming up with the idea to use a van with the sci-fi radar on the roof.

Customer: People are much too clever to fall for something like that now. But I imagine it had a lot of people running to the post office to get a licence back then.

Travellers (redefined)

7 May 2009

Customer: A Traveller was standing outside his caravan one morning at the side of a busy motorway. He was explaining to his young son that the people in the cars were going to work in the city. 'Some of them,' he said, 'have travelled miles. Maybe a two-hour commute each way, every day! They leave home early in the morning and get back very late at night. I've heard them say that they feel like they live in their cars!' There was silence for a moment while the little boy thought. Then he turned to his father and asked him: 'So why do they call us Travellers?'

Brilliant.

M50 mystery solved

8 May 2009

There has been a lot of speculation about the situation with the M50. Drivers have never seen anyone working on the new lanes. I drive by there myself regularly, and I don't remember ever seeing anyone working or driving any of the many abandoned-looking construction vehicles. The only difference from day to day is that some of the lanes are closed or divided temporarily using traffic cones. Anyway, I was cutting someone's hair the other day, and he explained the mystery . . .

Customer (a little annoyed): I was stuck on the car park again. I left work ages ago.

Barber: The car park?

Customer: The M50!

Barber: Very good! What's going on? I never see anyone working there.

Customer: It's the cutbacks. I heard there's only one lad working on it now.

Barber: Only one? You're joking. What does he do?
Customer: He works nights, rearranging the traffic cones!

Diverted funds

9 May 2009

I heard this many years ago. I was working close to the street where it happened, and many customers in the shop that week were talking about it.

In College Green, Dublin, there's a bank with a night safe outside, and this is where local businesses would lodge the day's takings. But one particular week it was out of order, and a big notice displaying that message hung in an official-looking way from the safe. It also instructed those who wished to lodge money to 'use the mobile safe in the van at the side of the road.' And many did, lodging the money and walking away. I heard this happened for three nights, although I can't say for sure.

Then, when someone checked their account, the money wasn't there. They called the bank and explained that they had followed all the instructions and had used the temporary safe in the van. 'What temporary safe?' was the shocking reply! Of course, there was nothing wrong with the real night-lodgement safe, and, alas, a lot of people were very skilfully conned.

A lot of money was stolen. The van pulled up outside when the bank closed in the evening, and the 'Out of order' sign was hung on the real night-lodgement safe. Then all that had to be done was to wait until the lodgements were made and drive away with the haul! I always thought it was probably the cleverest robbery I've ever heard about.

If I found a cure for baldness

10 May 2009

Customer: Whoever comes up with a cure for it will be a wealthy man. You wouldn't have to worry about money again if you found a cure for baldness.

Barber: Ah, I don't think they'll ever find a lotion that'll grow hair on a boiled egg.

Customer: And, if they did, sure you wouldn't want to get a drop of it on your hands, or you'd be like a werewolf!

Barber: Or, even worse, on her carpet!

Compulsive gambler

11 May 2009

A customer told me this while he was getting his hair cut. Everyone heard what he was saying, and as I looked round the shop everyone was smiling and holding back the laughter.

Customer: A friend of mine who buys lotto tickets all the time spends quite a lot of money every week. He has a bad habit, and he can't stop. He's always in the bookies, and he's always on the poker machines in town. The lads would tell you he has a problem. Sure he can't walk past a parking meter without putting money in it!

Murphy's Law

12 May 2009

Customer: I'm almost convinced there's a plausible argument to make Murphy's Law a proper, *bona fide* law of physics.

Barber: The 'what can go wrong will go wrong' law?

Customer: That's the one. You know, everybody's aware of it. I've seen children quote Murphy's Law when a piece of toast falls on the floor buttered-side down.

Barber: It's universal, all right. You should get someone to write it as an equation or formula that you could present to the science boffins.

Customer: Now that's not a bad idea.

Barber: If you get the Nobel Prize be sure to mention me!

Thinking big

13 May 2009

Customer: Did you see the lotto is worth six million tonight?

Barber: No, I didn't. Six million! Sure if I won that I could open my own barber shop!

First Indian manned space flight

14 May 2009

On the day of the first Indian manned space flight, in a bar in town an old man was served his pint by a foreigner. 'Where'd you get him from?' the oul' lad asked the head barman. 'Oh, he's from India.' The oul' lad sat quiet for a moment, then out of the blue he shouts out to the Indian: 'Hey, did you know one of your lads is in a rocket on the way to the moon just now?'

It brought the house down.

Waiter, there's a ring in my soup

15 May 2009

A waiter who worked in town told me this story while I cut his hair one day:

A young man, who intended to impress his girlfriend and propose to her, brought her to a very fancy restaurant in town. They were shown to their table, and herself was very impressed with the grandeur of the place. The waiter poured the wine as they decided what to order.

They went with the soup to start, and the waiter had been asked earlier to put a diamond ring into the girl's soup. The soup was served, and the young man was trying to keep a straight face at the thought of his true love finding a ring at the bottom of the bowl. But after taking a spoonful she suddenly had a terrifying look in her eyes and began to gasp, grabbing her throat and banging the table with her other hand. 'Oh my God,' said her boyfriend. 'She's choking.'

The waiter, quickly realising what had happened, ran to the table and grabbed the damsel in distress—who was now standing up—and began to administer the Heimlich manoeuvre in front of the shocked diners. Indeed, she had swallowed the ring, and it had lodged in her throat; but the waiter was able to dislodge it. She was mortified and in tears. Not in form for sitting through a meal, the two left the restaurant.

I wonder if they ever got married in the end.

Trim his eyebrows

16 May 2009

A woman comes into the shop . . .

Woman: My husband is on his way in, and I want you to trim his eyebrows. They're terribly long. Don't tell him, just cut them, and please don't tell him I was in here asking, or he'll be embarrassed.

Barber: Okay, don't worry. We can do that.

Woman: Oh, thanks.

And she left. Over the next few minutes, about three customers came in and sat down.

Customer: (whose hair I was cutting): You'll just have to cut everyone's eyebrows now!

Barber: Can you imagine? They'll all be saying to themselves, 'I'm never going back there again. They cut my eyebrows without even asking!'

Brendan Behan's cat trick

17 May 2009

I was cutting a painter's hair one day when he told me that Brendan Behan had been a painter also. He told me this story:

Customer: Behan was painting a sitting-room in a large house in Dublin. The room had a beautiful and expensive Persian rug that almost covered the entire floor. Well, Behan had been drinking the previous night and didn't feel too good, but he set up his ladder and began to paint. He was on the ladder with the pot of paint on the top step when he accidentally knocked over the pot, and it fell to the floor onto the rug, and the paint spilled out. The rug was destroyed! He knew he was in trouble now, as he heard someone approaching after hearing the noise of the pot hitting the floor. Suddenly he saw a cat, and he grabbed it and rolled it in the spill and let it go. It ran out the door, leaving a trail of paw marks in paint as it went. At the same moment there was a slight yelp from a maid who'd heard the noise. The cat had startled her, and, as she walked in and saw the mess, her jaw dropped. Behan shouted, 'That damn cat knocked my paint over.' Behan, thanks to his quick thinking, had passed the blame on, and the owner of the house even bought him a new pair of overalls.

Barber: That's a great story.

Customer: Yeah, for one man he was some man!

Tinfoil highlights

18 May 2009

Customer: Would you not cut women's hair?

Barber: Why do you say that?

Customer: Sure there must be a fortune to be made in that game. Huh? The wife went to a place in town, one of those big places, to get the foil and a cut.

Barber: The foil?

Customer: Ah, yeah. You know the foil they put on the hair with the colour in it?

Barber: Oh, yeah, tinfoil highlights—very expensive.

Customer: Expensive? I nearly passed away when she told me how much they were, and then she says the cut was extra on top of that. Jaysus, are they mad or what? The neighbour asked the missus the other day if she'd had a bad fright. She was looking funny at the wife for a minute, like there was something different about her, but she couldn't put her finger on it. 'Are you okay, Mary?' says she. 'You look like you had a scare.' 'No,' says the wife. 'God, do you know,' says the neighbour, realising what it was, 'it's your hair, Mary—it's turned grey!' You'd want to have seen her face!

Oestrogen in the water!

19 May 2009

I was talking to a customer one day about the new haircuts that teenagers wear and how feminine they seemed, and he began to tell me about a documentary he'd seen on television.

Customer: I saw a programme on TV about oestrogen in the water, and it's affecting the fish. In some of the big cities you see they recycle the water over and over for drinking. Although they can get rid of almost every pollutant and bacteria, they haven't been able to get rid of the oestrogen. So it's been affecting the fish, and they're changing sex!

Barber: I did hear about beef that's been injected with growth hormones—men can grow breasts if they eat a lot of it.

Customer: That's exactly it. Well, I was at a wedding recently, and I went outside for a cigarette. And what did I see: the women were all over on one side smoking, and on the other side the men were all holding the babies, and straight away, you know—right then and there I thought of the fish!

There's always one
20 May 2009

There was a lad who every now and again would pop his head in the door to tell us he was going next door for his prescription. Next door is an off-licence. He'd pass on the way back, waving a brown paper bag in the air for us to see. 'I got my prescription. I'll be feeling better tomorrow.' Sometimes he'd just shout in the odds the bookies were giving that day on anything from the chance of snow to the US presidential election. One day, when he'd just given us an update on the economy (in his own very original way), and had gone on about his business, the customer in my chair announced, 'There's one in every village!'

Everyone burst out laughing!

Microwave-seal test
21 May 2009

Customer: Do you know how to test a microwave oven to make sure the seals are working?

Barber: No, how?

Customer: You put a mobile phone in the oven and close the door. Don't turn the microwave on, though. Then you ring the phone in the oven, and if it rings then it's receiving a microwave signal from outside, and you know the seals are leaking!

Sacred cheese

22 May 2009

A lad from a local deli with a great sense of humour told me they had a new range of cheese in stock from Jerusalem. 'From Jerusalem?' I asked. 'Yeah, Cheeses of Nazareth!'

Jaws

23 May 2009

I was talking to a pensioner one day about films. We discussed James Bond for a while, and he mentioned all his favourites.

Customer: Sean Connery was the man—a real ladies' man. There was a big lad in some of the films—he had metal teeth, and he was much taller than Bond. He'd have been in the Roger Moore films. What was his name? I can't remember . . .

I could see him trying hard to recall the name, and I knew who he was talking about, so I told him.

Barber: It was Jaws.

Customer: Ah, no, no, that was a different film. That was about a fish.

Cobblers

25 May 2009

Customer: Do you cut your family's hair?

Barber: No, I cut hair all day, so when I go home I rarely pick up a scissors.

Customer: Well, you know what they say: cobblers' children have no shoes.

Bob Monkhouse

26 May 2009

Customer: I never liked that that Bob Monkhouse fella.

Barber: Same here—don't like a lot of those old-school English comedians.

Customer: After Bob Monkhouse died they showed some clips of interviews and jokes on Sky News, and he had this great joke that cracked me up. He'd said in an interview, 'They laughed when I said I was going to be a comedian. Well, they're not laughing now.'

'Wonderwall'

27 May 2009

While I was cutting hair one day, the Oasis song 'Wonderwall' was on the radio in the background.

Barber: Hey, there's 'Wonderwall' on the radio. Sounds as good as ever.

Customer: Did you hear the Ryan Adams version of it?

Barber: Yeah, I thought it was great.

Customer: A friend of mine was at the Ryan Adams gig in the Olympia, and in the middle of the gig someone shouts out, 'Play "Summer of '69"!' He wasn't impressed!

Out of shape

28 May 2009

While I was cutting a customer's hair one day he was telling me that he had decided it was high time he got fit. His friends, who were in the shop waiting, kept mocking his resolution to get healthy. He told me at one stage that he was going to start hiking up mountains, which resulted in everyone laughing in disbelief, and one of his friends shouted out, 'Be serious, John, you'd get altitude sickness walking up a stairs!'

Snow everywhere!

29 May 2009

Customer: My friends and I were trapped in the airport because of the heavy snow back in February. The whole airport was shut down by the heaviest snowfall in years. We only had one week off, and we were in the airport for days. We never got away in the end. It was a disaster!

Barber: Were you going somewhere sunny?

Customer: No, we were going skiing!

Barber: The irony!

A black eye from Fianna Fáil

31 May 2009

A customer with a very obvious black eye sat in the next barber's chair.

Barber: What happened to your eye?

Customer: I was walking home the other night, the night the wind was howling, and one of the Fianna Fáil election posters blew off a pole and hit me in the face!

Everyone in the shop cracked up laughing.

Hopeless case
1 June 2009

Customer (with wild curly hair): I'm looking to do something different. It's a real mess, isn't it?

Barber: Well, that's putting it mildly.

Customer: So what would you do if it was your hair?

Barber: I'd put a match to it!

Showjumping, Tallafornia style
2 June 2009

Customer: I was called out to an accident in Tallaght the other day. There was a kid riding a horse bareback, and he ran the horse at railings at the side of the road, trying to jump the rails. Well, the railings were too high for the horse, and there were spikes at the top. The horse got caught on the top of the railings!

Barber: My God, that's terrible. Was the kid okay?

Customer: Yeah, he was thrown clear, but the horse died. It was bleeding badly when I got there. Some corporation workmen were shovelling soil over the blood that was running out onto the road. They didn't have enough soil, and one of the men spotted a load of sand on the garden of a nearby house—they later found out it was for building a wall—and they ran over to get a few shovelfuls to throw onto the blood. There were three of them in the garden, digging their shovels in, when a window opened on the first floor. Staring out at them stood an angry woman with rollers in her hair, and she roared down to the lads below, 'You're not burying that horse in my bleedin' garden!'

Just looking!

3 June 2009

Customer: I was up at a garage, looking at the cars. There are some really nice second-hand cars going for a song at the moment. So I ask this guy who was working there how much the car I was looking at cost. 'That one is €16,599—it's a great car!' he tells me. So I say, '€16,599? I was down here yesterday, and the other guy said it was €16,399.' The dealer stared at me for a minute, like he was about to lose his cool, having been put on the spot, and said, 'Well, are you going to buy it or what?' I couldn't believe his attitude. I'm staring him right in the eye, and I say, 'I just want to know how much it is!'

Real estate

4 June 2009

Customer: I was in Galway last week—had a great time.

Barber: It's a great spot. I hear about it all the time— and don't forget the Galway girls!

Customer: During the property boom, you know, some parts of Galway became as expensive as top property in Dublin, and the estate agents started calling it G4!

The way we were

5 June 2009

Customer: I remember how bad it was in Dublin in the eighties. It really was impoverished, and the streets were filthy. There was litter everywhere. I was taking some Chinese businessmen into the city centre for a meeting, and they were silent in the car, looking out the windows as we were going down the quays. They were obviously shocked by the state of the place. Then one of them asks me, 'Is this because of the Troubles?'

B&Q

6 June 2009

A customer told me that a friend of his was in the North shopping, and he asked someone if there was a B&Q in Belfast. The man stared at him for a moment in disbelief and then said, 'A B and Q in Belfast? Where did you learn to spell?'

Yasmina and Kate

7 June 2009

Comments on the English television series 'The Apprentice'.

Customer: Did you see 'The Apprentice' last night?

Barber: Yeah, I was watching it. Really surprised Kate was in the final, but she was great. Her presentation was very good—didn't know her profit margin, though.

Customer: Yasmina was a serious contender from the early days, though. Kate didn't get going till later.

Barber: So you think he picked Yasmina based on the overall performance?

Customer: Either that or Sir Alan was thinking he couldn't pick the good-looking one!

More Yasmina and Kate

8 June 2009

Customer: I couldn't believe the job Yasmina got, putting TV screens up in hospitals to sell advertising on. I mean, that's not cool. Did you see her face when he told her?

Barber: I know, she was stunned. I was stunned. Sir Alan is head of such a large corporation, and Yasmina went through hell to win, and then she gets to sell advertising on TV screens? That's what my brother does, and he didn't win anything!

A great weekend

9 June 2009

Customer: That was the best June weekend. I remember it was 29 degrees. It makes such a difference to your mood. You'd forget all your worries—well, most, anyway!

Barber: I know. It's weather like that that makes me wish I was unemployed!

Customer: I'd be careful who you say that to if I were you!

The joy of repetition

10 June 2009

A customer told me a story of how he had worked many years ago behind the bar in a small country pub in Ireland.

The pub was always quite busy at the end of the week, and during his first week there he was taken aback by the reaction in the pub when the Angelus came on the radio at six o'clock. All the lads removed their caps and sat up, conversations stopped and pints were untouched as they all muttered the Angelus under their breath.

After he had been working there for a while he decided to record the Angelus and play it the next day one hour later, at seven, for a laugh. The tape was loaded, and the lads had been drinking. The real Angelus bells rang out at six. The pub stopped, and the few minutes were passed in quiet prayer. So at seven he played the recorded Angelus, and the exact same thing happened: all the men round the bar removed their caps and made the sign of the cross and began to murmur under their breath. He was biting his lip to stop himself laughing out loud. It was like a scene from 'Father Ted'!

Baltimore, Co. Cork—what a place!

11 June 2009

Customer: I was down in Baltimore in west Cork for the weekend. Great place.

Barber: I hear it's great in summer. There's a pub called Bushe's that people mention a lot.

Customer: Yes, I was there one night when one of the local people I was talking to told me Jeremy Irons has a castle nearby, and then a helicopter went over the bay. The lad I was talking to announced to everyone with a big grin on his face, 'That's Jeremy Irons going off to collect his Chinese takeaway.'

The Western burqa

12 June 2009

I was talking to an Islamic customer about the burqa. (There was a lot of discussion about it in the media at the time.) He told me that Western women wear a burqa too. 'No they don't,' I said. 'Yes they do,' he said. 'It's called Max Factor.'

Aslan

14 June 2009

I was talking to a customer who had recently renovated his pub and added a new music venue at the back, and he was talking to me about getting bands in to play.

Barber: How about Aslan? They always pull a large crowd.

Customer: Aslan? Ah, no—they're a plastic-glass gig!

Unibrow

15 June 2009

Customer: Will you trim the eyebrows for me, please? My daughter is calling me unibrow.

Barber: No problem.

Customer: I can't do them myself, as I wear glasses and I can't see the eyebrows in the mirror with them on 'cause they cover them up, and if I take the glasses off, well, I'm back to square one.

Barber: Well, if you could see without the glasses it's still not easy, as everything is backwards in a mirror, and you're using a scissors near your eye. You could do yourself an injury!

Customer: Dangerous things, those eyebrows!

New aftershave for Travellers
16 June 2009

Customer: Did you hear about the new aftershave for Travellers?

Barber: No, what's it called?

Customer: Howrya, boss!

Due decorum
17 June 2009

Customer (an older gent): Your birthday is coming up soon, isn't it?

Barber: It's at the end of the month. You have a great memory!

Customer: We must celebrate with due decorum!

Barber: Due decorum? What's that, a liqueur?

Downloading music
19 June 2009

Customer: Did you know it's morally okay to illegally download Amy Winehouse's and Pete Doherty's music?

Barber: Why?

Customer: Because if you paid for it they'd only spend your money on drugs!

A smoking gun

20 June 2009

Customer (a guard): Years ago I was driving home after work, and I was involved in a crash. I took a while to come round, and when I did I thought I'd been shot!

Barber: Why did you think that?

Customer: Because the airbags use gunpowder to discharge, and when I came round and was semi-conscious I got this really strong smell of gunpowder, and the first thing that went through my mind was that I'd been shot!

Barber: That would put a few years on you!

Witty banner

21 June 2009

Customer: I was in town earlier, and there was a march on over the pension levy.

Barber: Oh, yeah, I heard on the news. Was there a large turnout?

Customer: Yes, there was—more than I expected. Took me ages to get down the street, but there was a banner I saw that had on it 'Two Brians and no brains!'

Goodbye, Greens

22 June 2009

Customer: Hey, the Greens were wiped out in the election. We won't have to live in tree houses and knit our own yoghurt now! They had mad ideas, those fascists. Sure there was one in England saying people should only have one or two children, otherwise their carbon footprint would be too big. My God, hello, China, one-child policy and all that!

Barber: Well, Cowen has brought that in without anyone realising. Now that the economy has crashed, who can afford more than one child?

Customer: True, true. Well, now that the Green Party has lost some seats, and we can keep our light-bulbs, we might start to get our good weather back. Hello, global warming! Here comes the summer!

Frost/Nixon, Cowen/Lenihan
24 June 2009

Customer: My God, what sort of people are running this country? People would get behind the Government more and accept the cuts if the leaders themselves took a cut and made an effort. But there they were on the radio the other day, and they were caught playing golf instead of being at work.

Barber: I agree. Where's Cowen lately? They're calling him the Virtual Taoiseach.

Customer: You know, his plan wasn't so bad, but he couldn't sell it to us. I don't ever remember him explaining it. I only heard about it on BBC Radio 4. After the budget, the BBC had a report about the fact that Cowen had gone the opposite way to the US and the UK, and they were watching us to see how we'd get on.

Barber: How do you mean the opposite way?

Customer: Well, the US and UK were lowering interest rates and VAT. They were also printing money in the US and borrowing huge amounts to keep everything moving and people spending. In Ireland we had no real choice but to tax everyone just so the Government could keep the lights on and pay the wages. We are borrowing money, but Cowen and Lenihan are trying to minimise the amount, and the idea is we live like this until the wind changes and the economy begins to recover. Then, when it does, we'll have less of a debt and less to pay back, leaving us in a stronger position. It's a good plan. But, like I said, I heard all about it on BBC4! I think Cowen has a bit of the Nixon syndrome.

Barber: What's the Nixon syndrome?

Customer: Didn't you see *Frost/Nixon*? Great film. Nixon didn't like people much, and he didn't like having to explain himself.

Barber: In this day and age it's hard to understand how there's still such a lack of communication skills in Irish politics.

Customer: It's all gone to hell in a dustcart!

Off your trolley

25 June 2009

Not long ago the stories of hospital corridors filled with patients on trolleys awaiting treatment moved everyone in the country. But, as is always the case even in the darkest places, there is humour. An elderly man told me that while he was in hospital on a trolley in a corridor he spoke of how much of an ordeal it was and how embarrassed he felt. 'Would you believe, they gave me an injection on the trolley in front of everyone! No curtain—nothing,' he told me. 'I wouldn't mind, you know, only they had to give me the injection in the arse!' He praised the nurses and the families who came to visit other patients and who would always oblige by getting a drink or a cup of tea for a total stranger on a nearby trolley.

He told me about one particular character who had kept the patients' spirits up by cracking jokes and had kept them all laughing. 'At one stage your man renamed the corridor the Mary Harney Ward.'

Another customer told me that a patient got up off his trolley to go to the toilet only to come back and find someone else on it! And that was before the recession.

Whacko

27 June 2009

Barber: I can't believe Michael Jackson is dead. It's like a hoax or something to promote the tour. Maybe he'll be resurrected in three days. It's the kind of thing he'd do!

Customer: Michael Jackson? Sure he's a Charlie Chester!

Barber: Well, that was never proved, but he's brown bread now.

Customer: Or white bread!

Haughey's PR

28 June 2009

A customer was talking about political scandal, and Charlie Haughey came up in the conversation.

Customer: Whoever looked after Haughey's press was

very good, you know.

Barber: What makes you say that?

Customer: Well, it was a long time ago, but Haughey was big into horses, and one day, while he was at the stables, he met a young lady. The story goes that he ended up in one of the stables with her and made a move on her. She began to scream, and her father and brother, who were close by, ran in to see what was wrong. They found a startled Haughey in the stable and cornered him. A punch-up ensued, two against one, and Charlie didn't come out so well. Anyway, the next day Haughey was pictured in the papers with his injuries, and the PR story was that he had fallen from his horse, which was a good cover up, but the giveaway was that in the picture he had a black eye!

Barber: Is that a true story?

Customer: I heard it myself!

Johnny Depp's sunglasses

29 June 2009

One of the lads I worked for cut Johnny Depp's hair for a film that was never finished, as it ran out of finance early on. It was a good few years ago now. I think Marlon Brando was in it also. But I remember a story he told me about Johnny Depp having a pair of sunglasses that everyone was talking about, and wondering where he got them. My friend brought it up in conversation when he was cutting Johnny's hair and asked him if they were designer, which, to his surprise, Johnny found funny. 'I was travelling around America by car,' Johnny said, 'and I pulled into a gas station and filled the tank up, and when I was paying for the gas the attendant handed me the glasses, so I asked her, "What are these for?" And she said, "They're free with a fill of gas," and I've had them ever since.'

You just never know!

Girls do it better

1 July 2009

Customer: Girls are outperforming boys in exams and at college this last ten years. It seems they're more suited to being academics. The boys just can't get down to it the same way.

Barber: Girls just seem to realise what's expected of them while the lads even at Junior Cert age are still dreaming of being football stars!

BOD

2 July 2009

Customer: I must say I really admire Brian O'Driscoll. I mean, he gets injured repeatedly. Sometimes he gets terrible injuries, and then when he plays his next game he goes at it without concern, putting himself in harm's way time after time, like he'd never been injured. He must have no fear.

Barber: It's impressive, all right. After the Rugby World Cup I heard a doctor say the injuries players get at that level are similar to the injuries he'd normally see treating patients who'd been in a car crash!

Summer job

4 July 2009

Customer: My young lad just started working in Tesco for the summer.

Barber: Tesco? What's he doing there?

Customer: Learning Polish!

Periwinkle-smugglers

5 July 2009

After the film *The Wind That Shakes the Barley* came out, older customers who had seen it began to open up, and some of them told me stories they'd long forgotten.

Customer (a great customer who was in his late eighties when he told me this): My friends and I were coming home through the [Dublin] city centre. We were all about eleven or twelve. We had been collecting periwinkles near Ringsend, and we didn't notice the time. Back then everyone had to be off the streets by nine o'clock, and the Black and Tans were out enforcing the curfew. We gathered so many periwinkles that we had to put them onto the front of our jumpers and then hold the bottom of the jumper up in front of us like a pouch. Two Black and Tans saw us and asked us what we had in our jumpers. We were terrified. 'Periwinkles,' we told them, and they got annoyed because they didn't know what they were. The Tans ordered us to spread them out on the street, and we emptied them all out of our jumpers onto the ground. They had never seen or heard of cockles, and I suppose they thought we had something hidden amongst them. They let us go, but we were lucky—we could have been killed.

Barber: It's hard to even imagine what life must have been like back then!

Bad things happen in threes . . .

6 July 2009

I've heard this so often that it's beyond coincidence. As soon as I mention that the car has broken down or that the mobile phone is acting up, most every customer will say, 'Only one more to go, then' or 'Well, that's two out of three.' It does seem to apply to major disruptions in our lives—like deaths in the circle of friends and family—that, within a few days, or the space of a month at most, three large life interruptions occur consecutively. Perhaps this unquantified law of the social world is a close relative of Murphy's Law?

Antiques

7 July 2009

Customer: That's a very nice cut-throat razor. Is it an antique?

Barber: It is. I don't use it now. It's just for show. It's Victorian, I think.

Customer (holding up my takeaway coffee): And this coffee cup?

Barber: I'd say this is Cardboardian!

Bank shares

8 July 2009

Customer: Had the kids round at my dad's house at the weekend. He lost all his savings in the crash, so he's a bit down. He was counting out his loose change for the kids, and I was standing beside him when he says to them, 'Now off you go down to the shops and get yourselves some penny sweets. Or, if you want,' he says under his breath, 'you could buy most of my bank shares.'

Rock gods play golf!

9 July 2009

Customer: I was reading a book Alice Cooper wrote about golf! Can you believe back in the eighties Iggy Pop and Cooper used to quietly slip out of rock and roll parties before midnight so they could be up early and be out on the golf course by 7 a.m. They played thirty-six holes at the crack of dawn so no-one would see them. At that time they feared it would damage their 'wild men of rock, serial killer' image.

Barber: How did they get into golf?

Customer: Cooper was drinking heavily in the early eighties, and he almost died. He was drinking whiskey for breakfast and a case of beer to follow! So he quit the drink and started playing golf. He says it saved his life. Don't know how Iggy started, though!

Classified ads

10 July 2009

Customer: I've had a terrible few weeks! My mate's put an ad in the men-seeking-men classifieds online, and they put my phone number up too!

Barber: That's mad. Did anyone ring you?

Customer: The phone never stopped at night. Two, three in the morning, lads asking if I was available! It was a nightmare! When I told my friends, they couldn't stop laughing. They thought it was a great laugh! The feckers!

The living dead

11 July 2009

Customer (a barman): An old man who was drinking at the bar handed me his newspaper and asked me if I'd look up the death notices for a Duffy, so I look through it quickly. 'No,' I say to him, 'there's no Duffy here.' 'Are you sure?' he says. 'Yes,' I said, handing him back his paper. 'Good,' said the oul' fella. 'I didn't know if I was dead or alive when I woke up this morning!'

On women

12 July 2009

Customer: Women? They're all great, until you get to know them!

Recession greetings

13 July 2009

Barber: How are you getting on?

Customer (sounding hopeless): Surviving. Sure there's no use in complaining. Sure no-one would listen anyway. At least I'm still breathing!

Barber: Did you have your money in bank shares, then?

Born in the wrong country

14 July 2009

Barber: Where are you from?

Customer: Mauritius. It's an island in the Indian Ocean.

Barber: Mauritius—that's like a paradise over there. Why did you come to Ireland, of all places?

Customer: I like the weather.

Barber: You like the weather? Are you serious?

Customer: Yeah, it's far too hot over there, and I don't have to worry about that here!

Barber: You're mad, you are!

More recession greetings

15 April 2009

Barber: How are you?

Customer: Better than the small farmer!

Double standards

16 July 2009

Customer: There's been a lot of crashes on the roads involving the Polish lately!

Barber: Yeah, there's been a few, all right.

Customer: And you know why, don't you?

Barber: No, why?

Customer: Ah, they drink and drive!

Space race
17 July 2009

Yesterday was the fortieth anniversary of the Apollo 11 moon landing, which came up in the shop and led to this comment . . .

Customer: During the space race they needed to invent a pen that could write in zero gravity, and it also had to write upside down. America spent millions of dollars and years of research making the pen while the Russians used a pencil!

The great mobile-phone conspiracy
20 July 2009

Customer: Whenever something big happens in the world, like the death of a celebrity, a plane crash—you know, an event that gets the headlines—there are relentless amounts of jokes being texted from one mobile to another.

Barber: A lot of people have mentioned it in the barber shop over the years, and people have often said that no-one knows who writes these jokes or where they come from originally. We just receive them and forward them to friends!

Customer: Well, there is a theory that there's a think-tank of specially chosen lads who all rush into a room as soon as there's major world news breaking, and they write these jokes and forward them to a circle of friends, who then forward the messages on to their friends, and the snowball begins to roll down the hill. The mobile-phone companies who stand by and watch the money roll in probably have them in an office somewhere, sworn to secrecy.

Barber: Well, if it's true, they're getting lazy, because the jokes—as a customer mentioned recently—are quite similar to jokes used for previous world news events—just the names or details are changed. Good theory, though!

Surf's up!

21 July 2009

Barber (to an Australian customer): I bet you miss surfing and Vegemite?

Customer: Miss surfing? No, most weekends I go down to the west coast and surf. It's really good here.

Barber: The surfing must be catching on here: lots of people are telling me they surf down the west!

Customer: I bet you didn't know you held the record for the most people surfing a wave at the same time: forty-four altogether! Back in May 2006.

By the way, I looked it up, and it's true. I also found that, in 1979, the Pro/Am Surfing World Championships were held in Easky, Co. Sligo!

Interrogation

23 July 2009

Barber: Are you off today?

Customer: No, just on a lunch break.

Barber: Oh, where do you work?

Customer: Just in an office up the road.

Barber: What sort of work do you do?

Customer: What is this, the sixty-second quiz?

Ireland's diaspora, interesting fact

24 July 2009

A customer was talking about Admiral William Brown (from Foxford in Co. Mayo), who is the father of the Argentine navy. So then he (the customer) tells me that a huge number of Irish people emigrated to Argentina. Not trusting the information, I looked it up, and here are some facts from the Diaspora web site:

In the latter half of the nineteenth century approximately 45,000 Irish people arrived in Argentina, some 20,000 of whom settled there, with most of the rest moving to the United States.

Today in Latin America some 300,000 to 500,000 people are estimated to have some Irish ancestry, most of them living in Argentina, with lesser numbers in Central America, Uruguay and Brazil.

Who would have thought it!

Bodyboards

25 July 2009

Customer (from New Zealand): Bodyboards—they're deadly dangerous. Do you know what we call them at home?

Barber: No, I've no idea.

Customer: Shark biscuits, mate!

Barber: Why do they call them that?

Customer: Because of the number of sharks that attack people on them. See, your hands and legs are paddling along, and from beneath the shark looks up and thinks it's a big turtle and goes in for his tea. So that's why we call them shark biscuits.

Great party the other night . . .

26 July 2009

In the shop one very busy Saturday afternoon a guy comes in to queue and sees a lad he knows having his hair cut. A conversation begins . . .

Customer *1:* Hey! Saw you at the party the other night!

Customer 2: Yeah, great one, wasn't it?

Customer 1: Who was that dog-ugly bird you were talking to all night?

Everyone in the shop started laughing.

Customer 2: That was my girlfriend.

You could have heard a pin drop . . .

Steak football

27 July 2009

Barber: Is it just an Irish thing? Why are we so hesitant
to complain in restaurants when food is not right?
People think if you send a steak back to the kitchen
the chefs will throw it on the floor, kick it around a
bit—if you're lucky—toss it back in the pan for a few
minutes and then send back out to you! Apart from
being the only one at the table to return your plate,
and everyone else in your company having a cringe
moment: 'Oh, for God's sake, don't be so fussy. My
food is fine,' and so on . . . Have you ever heard of
anything like that going on?

Customer (a chef): Yeah, I've seen it being done! There
are restaurants where you can be sure that this type of
attitude is not tolerated, but there are places where it
can happen.

Barber: Are you serious?

Customer: Well, say you're the chef and you're very
busy. You have cooked a steak and sent it out of the
kitchen, and it arrives back in at the behest of some
gobshite whose staple recession diet is cornflakes and
petrol-station sandwiches. The customer is telling an
experienced, fully qualified chef that what he has
prepared is not to their liking. And, hey, the kitchen
staff have a quick game of steak football before it goes
back in the pan. It depends on what sort of place
you're in.

Barber: So what would you do if your food wasn't up
to standard?

Customer: I'd get up and walk out of the restaurant.

Galway Races

28 July 2009

Customer: A friend of mine is at
the Galway Races. It's not as crazy as
it has been in the Celtic Tiger years.

Barber: It's still a big draw, though—just not as many
helicopters!

Customer: Yeah, he told me it was like Vietnam up
there with all the choppers a while ago. There were so
many people flying in they had to build a control
tower!

The Irish crown jewels

1 August 2009

A customer was having his hair cut, and I noticed that
he had a small paperback book with him that he'd
placed on the shelf.

Barber: What's that you're reading?

Customer: It's a book about the Irish crown jewels!

Barber: But there are no Irish crown jewels!

Customer: We had crown jewels in Ireland, but they
were stolen in 1907. One of the guards who looked
after the jewels in Dublin Castle disappeared after the
robbery but was seen with two men the night before in
the Shelbourne Hotel in Dublin. There was one jewel
in particular, a large emerald, said to be the largest in
the world. They were a serious collection of jewels!

Barber: Well, every day is a school day, and you learn
something new!

The dog knows

2 August 2009

Customer: When the doorbell rings at home the dog always runs to it, and the wife says the other day, 'Why does he always think it's for him!?'

Brendan Behan

3 August 2009

A customer told me this one today. It's a quotation from Brendan Behan. The customer said he drank with Brendan, although I seem to be meeting a huge number of people who were in the GPO in 1916 or who drank with Behan or Patrick Kavanagh—or, as one lad told me recently, who were seeing one of Kavanagh's girlfriends behind his back! So here's what Behan said: 'I was court-martialled in my absence and sentenced to death in my absence, so I said they could shoot me in my absence.'

Pensioners

4 August 2009

Sometimes a barber will mistakenly charge a pensioner full price if the customer happens to look younger than their actual age. This can cause a tense moment, but it is in fact a reverse compliment. It happened the other day.

Customer: Oh, I'm a pensioner. I can show you my card.

Barber: Sorry, I didn't realise you were on the OAP price. You look too young.

Customer: Low mileage and one careful owner.

The oul' fellas are so witty . . .

Lunsters

5 August 2009

Customer: You know the Leinster fans who follow Munster are called Lunsters?

Barber: I do.

Customer: Well, hazard a guess at what they call the Connaught fans who support Munster: Cunsters!

Bono's table

6 August 2009

A customer told me that his aunt was in a restaurant in Temple Bar, and during the course of her meal a waiter asked her if she'd mind moving tables, as Bono was coming in, and he always sat at the table she had chosen. She was a big fan, and so she didn't mind. Soon after she moved tables, Bono arrived with some friends. Later she spotted a tall, well-built man getting up from Bono's table and heading out for a cigarette, so she followed him and went out for a cigarette too. She struck up a conversation with him, thinking he was part of the security, and asked him if it would be okay to ask Bono for an autograph or a photo, and he said he didn't see why not. He told her to wait for him to bring her over and introduce her.

They went back to their tables, and, not long after,

the guy came over and said it would be okay to go over to meet Bono. She got her photos and an autograph and chatted for a while. She thanked them and went back to her table. A while later, Bono and Co. left, and she asked for the bill.

'Oh,' the waiter said, 'the gentleman at that table paid your bill,' pointing to Bono's table.

'Bono?' said the aunt in shock.

'No,' said the waiter, 'Bruce Springsteen, the guy who took you over to meet Bono.' And then it dawned on her that the man she thought was a bodyguard and who spoke to her while she was outside smoking was Bruce Springsteen!

The customer told me that his aunt had won a prize on a radio station for that story.

Strange shower
7 August 2009

Customer: I was doing a delivery in Ranelagh a while ago, and it was a lovely morning. The sun was shining, but as I looked down the street it was raining. But it was dry where I was! It was only about twenty feet away, and I was standing there in the sun. I never saw anything like it since.

Down and out—of the country!
10 August 2009

Wow, I've never heard so many stories of people's lives being turned upside down and inside out and then in the aftermath trying to make some sense of it all.

Well, I had a regular customer in, and he was stressed, but I must say he was in good humour— anxious, maybe, but he was feeling positive. He told me he had bought an apartment ten years ago, when things were beginning to move in the property market. He was on an average wage, but he had no dependants and was single. He let this city-centre property, and all was well. Later that year he was in the bank where he knew the staff and had his account and mortgage. The manager spoke to him and said, 'You're getting on well. Would you like to buy another apartment?'

My customer couldn't believe it. He thought about it and decided he could do it, and so apartment number two was purchased and let. About a year later the rates came down, and he found that he was now in profit every week. The rent was greater than the mortgage payments, and the bank offered him another mortgage. This went on for the next few years, until he had ten properties. To minimise the risk, he took the last half-dozen mortgages as interest only; being the sensible type he realised that what goes up must come down. He was doing well. What would these ten apartments be worth by the time he was ready to retire? They were worth more than three million now. All he had to do was keep them rented and pay the mortgages . . .

I looked at his expression in the mirror at this stage, and his face changed from that of a proud, self-driven speculator to that of a man whose luck had jack-knifed on the highway of life. He told me that this haircut was the last one he'd get in Ireland for a long time. He'd posted the keys of the ten apartments to the bank—the jingle post. The tenants were leaving, as he'd rented to immigrant workers who'd lost jobs and were going home. He had only a modest wage and couldn't supplement the mortgage payments. He was paying interest only, so even if he could sell a property he'd still owe the banks a huge chunk of change, as the properties were now worth little: two-thirds of the original price. He was leaving for America later that day. He told me how he'd be able to start from scratch there and that the bank couldn't pursue him for the money. He couldn't come back, of course.

I heard from a member of the staff of a local bank, while he was having his regular trim, that a lot of personal loans and car loans taken out around Christmas by immigrant workers would remain unpaid, as they had left the country and left their cars at the airport. This isn't just happening in Ireland, though. Irish and English construction workers leaving Dubai abandoned three thousand cars at the airport car park, some taking out a loan before leaving for home and maxing out their credit cards buying presents for family and friends.

So, now you know you have an option: when you get your next credit card bill, you can pay it—or leave the country!

Michael Collins

12 August 2009

I was talking to a customer one Saturday when the shop was very busy. It was back in 1996. I know that's a long time ago, but it came back to me today when I was telling a customer:

Barber: Did you hear *Michael Collins* is being released next week?

Customer: Michael Collins? I thought he was dead!

The entire shop erupted in laughter.

Credit card minimum-payment bill
13 August 2009

Barber: A lot of people are staying in a bit more to pay off loans and credit cards. They're not going out for lunch at work, so they're bringing in a packed lunch from home instead.

Customer (who works in a bank): I bet you didn't know it can take twenty-five years to pay back a card with a €2,000 balance if you pay the minimum amount only! In the States they're at present trying to pass a law so that the card-issuer must forewarn the card-holder of the true cost of credit.

Barber: That's really clever. It's like magic numbers: your card purchases turn into a mortgage!

U2 360 Croke Park
14 August 2009

Customer: I was at the U2 concert in Croke Park the other night. It was fantastic! I got shivers down my spine about six or seven times during the middle section of the show when U2 played one hit after another. All the classics back to back. They never let the crowd up for air!

Barber: Everyone I spoke to seemed to think it was spectacular. The stage alone was like one of the tripods from *The War of the Worlds*!

Customer: I wonder how the residents are getting on. They had blocked the U2 trucks, leaving in protest [over noise and disruption], and the trucks carrying the stage missed the ferry! The Hannover concert was pulled. It's in the paper today.

Barber: I saw that earlier. The promoters are suing the residents over the losses!

Customer: They only just got the grass back down in time for the all-Ireland!

Swine flu

15 August 2009

Customer: That swine flu is spreading. I hear there are a hundred people in hospital now.

Barber: Yeah, it was on the news earlier.

Customer: Well, I'll only start worrying if it gets worse than that Colombian flu they had in Tallaght a few years ago!

Phil Lynott

16 August 2009

I was talking about Phil Lynott to a customer one day. He told me this old story about his aunt at a big party—and, of course, Phil Lynott was there.

His aunt was a good-looking young woman. Phil singled her out soon after coming into the room and struck up a conversation. He began flirting with her, but she wasn't interested. He came closer to her and whispered something in her ear that would have shocked even the liberal-minded. The customer told me his aunt was horrified by this but remained composed and walked away as if she was bored. Phil was stunned: it probably didn't happen to him very often. Then the customer tells me that his aunt was in fact—although dressed in fashionable clothes—a nun! She just got time off from the convent for the party!

The words Phillo whispered in her ear must have haunted her for years!

The Aviva Stadium

17 August 2009

Customer: I see the Aviva is coming on well. The boxes aren't selling, though, probably because of the recession.

Barber: They're expensive too. Eamon Dunphy said they'll have to book the Rolling Stones to fill it!

The banks again . . .

18 August 2009

Customer: A friend of mine who works at one of the big banks told me that they all got golf and gym memberships, after us bailing them out!

Barber: Wow, if people hear about this there'll be trouble!

Customer: And they still have their corporate boxes at Croke Park!

You won't believe me if I tell you

20 August 2009

I heard this story a few times. My brother, who worked near the pub in question, knew the barman. It was a good few years ago . . .

In a pub in Naas it was just another ordinary day. There were a few locals drinking at the bar and four noisy lads in the back room playing pool and drinking. The barman would pull the pints and bring them in to the lads playing pool, and he had told them repeatedly to keep the noise down. Later they started singing, and after a while the barman shouted into the back room that if they kept it up he'd kick them all out. It went quiet for a few seconds, and then the lads in the back room burst out laughing! They were in hysterics.

The local people were dying to know who was in the back room, and one of them decided to go in and put money on the table to book the next game. He came back out laughing himself. 'So who's in there?' they asked. 'You won't believe me if I tell you,' he says. 'It's Mick Jagger, Bill Wyman, Keith Richards and Rod Stewart!'

Irish traffic lights

23 August 2009

A barman who works in a top hotel got to know an American couple who were on holiday. They told him they'd rented a car to see a bit of the countryside, and he didn't see them for a couple of days. When they got back after their trip they told the barman what a great time they had. The weather had been good for them, which made it all the better.

Later on, the woman asked the barman what was up with the traffic lights in Ireland.

'Why, what about them?' enquired the puzzled barman.

'They beep. Your traffic lights make a beeping noise,' the woman tells him.

'Oh, that. That's for the blind people. You know, so they know when the lights change.'

'Oh. You know, back home we don't let the blind people drive.'

Her husband was mortified!

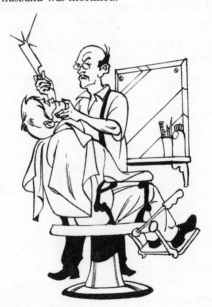

The demon barber!

26 August 2009

Things are only getting back to normal here in the barber shop. For quite some time when I'd go to use a cut-throat razor on a customer's neck they'd jump and say, 'No, don't use that!' So I'd ask why, and they'd say they had seen *Sweeney Todd* (the film about the mythical murderous barber). I'd have to leave the razor down and trim the hair with a clippers or scissors. But, as I said, it's been a few weeks now since a customer cringed in my chair, and it seems that the fear has subsided. So, sharpen the cut-throats—it's back to the close shaves.

The Malahide railway bridge collapse

27 August 2009

Customer: Did you hear about the railway bridge that collapsed in Malahide the other day?

Barber: I did. I saw the picture in the paper. They were lucky the train had just gone over the bridge and it fell in afterwards!

Customer: Well, CIE had to put buses on to transport people to work now that the bridge had collapsed, and this morning I heard the buses got into to town twenty-five minutes earlier than the train normally does!

Barber: So, no need to fix the bridge, then!

Directions in Ireland . . .

28 August 2009

Customer: I was travelling down to Carlow the other day, and I was trying to find the Dolmen Hotel. There were no signs anywhere that I could see, so I stopped and asked someone in the street.

Barber: I always feel sorry for tourists travelling in Ireland. I often wonder how they ever find their way round.

Customer: Well, this guy gives me the directions, and I say to him, 'How come there are no signs for the hotel?' And he says, 'Sure everybody knows where the Dolmen is!'

Witty Dublin place-names

29 August 2009

A customer was giving me directions to a place on the north side. (I ask customers sometimes, and I get great routes from sales reps.)

Customer: Take a right at the Donaghmede Opera House.

Barber: The what?

Customer: That's what it's known as locally. It's Tesco at Clare Hall!

Strange fashion . . .

31 August 2009

While we were talking about modern fashion and the 'youth of today', the subject of the wearing of jeans down low arose. You'll no doubt have seen lads wearing their jeans so low that their underwear shows. It's usually three to four inches below the normal waistline.

Barber: A young lad who comes into the shop wears his jeans really low, and he told me he has to walk funny to keep them from falling down.

Customer: Do you know where that whole fashion came from?

Barber: No, I've no idea.

Customer: In the States, when a gang are arrested and the police lock them up they take their belts so they can't hang themselves or beat each other up swinging the belts in the cells and hitting each other with the buckles. When they're released they all walk out with no belts and their jeans hanging down low, and, because gangster culture is 'cool', the kids copy the look.

Can't wait for tomorrow!

1 September 2009

When I finished a customer's hair today and had shown him the back in the mirror he looked quite pleased . . .

Customer: That's great. Now I can't wait until tomorrow.

Barber: Why tomorrow?

Customer: 'Cause I'm getting better looking every day!

L'Oréal economics

2 September 2009

Customer: I can't get over how everyone is in such debt with personal loans and credit cards and negative equity. It just shows how most people were borrowing money just to subsidise their lifestyle, and they justified it all with L'Oréal economics.

Barber: L'Oréal economics?

Customer: You know, 'Because I'm worth it.'

Euro-style

3 September 2009

Customer: I was walking round town last week near Grafton Street. I was off, and the weather was great—warm and sunny. Now, I hadn't been in town for a long time, and, as I looked around, you know, I couldn't believe it. There were street entertainers, people sitting outside coffee shops and bars, talking and reading papers, and I thought to myself [he says in all seriousness]: 'You'd think you were in Europe!'

Classic.

The writing's on the wall

5 September 2009

A customer told me today that Mary Coughlan, Brian Lenihan and Brian Cowen are now referred to as the 'drinks cabinet'.

A creamy pint of black

6 September 2009

A barman told me this one. One of them should write a book: they always seem to have great stories!

Customer (the barman): Had a tour of Americans in the other day. I was handing out a few pints of Guinness. One of the Americans was watching and came up to the bar and said, 'That looks real good! Hey, I'll have to try a pint of your Guinness, now that I'm here in Ireland. But can I get one without the cream? I'm lactose intolerant.'

An expert at partitions?

7 September 2009

An older, well-spoken gentleman was describing the haircut he wanted.

Customer: Can I get a partition there on the left?

Barber: A partition?

Customer: Yes, you're an expert at partitions, aren't you?

Barber: The only experts on partitions I know of are Moses and Michael Collins. I think you mean a parting.

Dry hair

8 September 2009

Customer: The girlfriend says my hair is like a dry Weetabix!

Barber: It is too!

Jekyll-and-Hyde weather

9 September 2009

Customer: What's going on with the weather! We've had another bad summer, and the Met Office said it would be good. From day to day they consistently get it wrong.

Barber: There's just no accountability in the Met Office, and if the people who tell us the weather keep getting it wrong they should be fired. Three wrong forecasts and they're out. That should be the way, and it would make it more interesting for the rest of us.

Customer: Three strikes and they're out! I think a trapdoor would be great too: everyone would be watching the forecast then. Did you hear about that lad who forecasts using the sun spots? He's said the weather will be great from the 7th to the 21st, I think, so we'll see if he's right next week.

Barber: It should be good, because the kids are back at school—you know, Murphy's Law and all that. The Met Office said his method is like reading tea leaves in a cup, so I'm told. There's no science involved.

Customer: It's raining again. Look [pointing out the window], the sun was shining a minute ago. It's Jekyll-and-Hyde weather out there!

Even your tractor isn't safe!

10 September 2009

Customer: Did you hear the banks called in the loans they'd given farmers to buy tractors?

Barber: No, I didn't.

Customer: Well, down the country they went around repossessing them. Some farmers had only two or three years left to pay off. But they got their own back, as they filled the tanks with acid and sand, so they're totally useless. The banks can't sell them off at auction.

Barber: When you think it's us the public, farmers and all that who backed the guarantee that's kept them open for business, and this is how they repay the people. Can't they give us some time to get back on our feet before they come knocking for your house, your car or your tractor?

Customer: It just shows how desperate they are for cash

flow. They're auctioning off cars all the time for a fraction of their worth, just to get some money in. My guess is they're still in trouble. There's still the threat— a rumour I hear a lot—that one of the major banks will go under in the new year.

Far and Away

13 September 2009

The film *Far and Away,* with Tom Cruise and Nicole Kidman, was made in Ireland, and a lot of the New York set was filmed on the cobbled streets of Temple Bar. There were lots of jokes going round in the pubs in the evening when the cast and crew had wrapped up. I remember someone in the Temple Bar pub with a plastic milk crate telling people that it was the one Tom Cruse stood on when he was in a scene with Nicole so he'd be the same height as her.

Anyway, this story is true, as I was there myself, and I met some of the regular Saturday customers there. The Boston scenes at the end of the film were shot around Fitzwilliam Square in Dublin, and they needed to cover everything in snow, as it was supposed to be the depths of winter in Boston. This was achieved by spraying some chemical compound over the houses and the streets, and it really looked like snow. It even stuck together like snow, much to the delight of the folk coming home from Leeson Street's clubs in the early hours, who found a winter wonderland around the corner, and in their mildly merry state it was an invitation to mayhem.

As soon as people realised that they could make snowballs from this 'snow' it was like a school yard at break time. There were snowballs flying everywhere and more and more people joining in as they came down the street. It was total chaos. I met a couple of guys I knew who were regulars in the barber shop, and they showed me a snowman they'd made that was even wearing a scarf one of the lads had donated. I'd say that at the height of it more than a hundred people had been involved in the snowball fight.

The next day, when the film crew arrived, the set was destroyed, and at great expense they had to respray the entire set with fresh fake snow. The next night, clubbers were looking forward to another snowball fight in Fitzwilliam Square, but this time there were a number of guards along the street. Although everyone was disappointed that there wasn't going to be a snowball fight, one of the lads, who was a bit worse for wear, shouted out to one of the guards, 'So what are you doing here?' And the guard replied, 'We're guarding the snow.'

Well, I don't need to tell you that people were in tears laughing!

A new style

14 September 2009

Customer: Can I have a carpet, please?
Barber: You'll have to go to Des Kelly's for that. We just cut hair!

Turns out he wanted a crop.

Time machine

16 September 2009

Customer: There's a story out there that the hadron collider is so dangerous to humanity and the planet that it's being sabotaged.

Barber: I never heard anything about that. I did hear lots of talk about the world ending when it was turned on. So who's trying to sabotage it?

Customer: [whispers] People from the future!

Barber: Like Terminator?

Customer: Exactly.

Dino's Bar and Grill

18 September 2009

Customer: You know that line in the song there [Phil Lynott was playing on the radio in the shop] where he says, 'Down at Dino's Bar and Grill'?

Barber: I do. Why?

Customer: Well, that's a chipper in Terenure. They have a picture of Phillo up on the wall too. He used to get chips there. It was Dino's for years, but it's a new name now—can't remember. But look for the one with the Phil Lynott picture on the wall.

The spud

19 September 2009

Customer: You know the potato isn't indigenous to Ireland? It was brought to England by Sir Walter Raleigh. He lived here for some time and is said to have planted the first potatoes here! It was grown in

Chile and Peru—the Incas were big potato-eaters. Since before the Famine it's been a staple food, and we're almost defined by it: Guinness and potatoes!

Barber: I can't believe it. The spud is an immigrant!

The wit of George Bernard Shaw

20 September 2009

Customer: George Bernard Shaw received a letter from a young lady. I was told she was a model, but nevertheless she was well known in Dublin social circles at the time. She wrote to Shaw in the hope that he might marry her, and she very cleverly added that with her looks and his brains they would have beautiful, intelligent children. Shaw wrote back: 'I must decline your tempting invitation, on the basis that the children might be born with my looks and your brains.'

'Just a Minute': The sixty-second quiz

22 September 2009

Customer: Hearing that [a clip of Larry Gogan on the radio] reminds me. A friend of mine told me there was a book with all the funny wrong answers from the sixty-second quiz.

Barber: I guess it's just another urban myth. It'd be a great one, though.

Customer: Best one I heard was Larry asks the contestant to complete the saying 'As happy as . . .' and he can't get it, so Larry gives him a clue and says, 'Think of my name,' and your man says, 'a pig in shite!'

Barber: I love the one where he says, 'What star do travellers follow?' and the guy says, 'Joe Dolan!'

Charlie Chaplin in Co. Kerry

23 September 2009

A customer from Waterville told me this story.

Charlie Chaplin was a regular visitor to Co. Kerry, in particular to Waterville, where there's a bronze statue of him. He would arrive in a hotel and set up his projector and put the word out that he was going to show films on a big screen. He attracted a large crowd of all ages and would show selections from his films and private film of Hollywood. As you can imagine, it would have been nirvana to any film buff.

So everyone would arrive in the evening, and the kids would be sent in to watch the films. The adults were nowhere to be seen. They were of course in the hotel bar for the night. So Charlie ended up babysitting, but he didn't seem to mind. He did it many times and would show films over an entire weekend. Maybe he even inspired a few budding directors.

On Bertie's re-election in 2007

24 September 2009

Customer (a pensioner): I've no time for that Bertie fella. It was the women of Ireland who voted him back in after he turned on the waterworks on TV.

Barber: I remember hearing about him shedding a tear in the interview. I haven't seen it, though.

Customer: Just as well. It's shameful! I've no time for a lad who plays the victim to get what he wants!

Bushy sideburns

26 September 2009

Customer: Will you trim the Brillo Pads there? Keep them long but not so bushy.

More on Bertie

3 October 2009

Customer: Bertie was a good housekeeper. He kept things ticking over, but we needed a lot more.

Barber: Yeah, we needed a Taoiseach!

The Lisbon Treaty (round two)

4 October 2009

Customer: Did you see Michael O'Leary and Eamon Dunphy were calling for a Yes vote?

Barber: I had a lad tell me he was voting Yes because it's so much easier going on holidays with the euro currency!

Customer: Jaysus. There's all sorts out there. Well, I'm voting Yes because there's no-one to lead us out of the bankruptcy we've found ourselves in. When things were good here during the Celtic Tiger days the health system was crumbling and education needed more cash to build schools—there are still many rented prefab schools around the country. Industry was ignored. The main business being done was in construction. This is particularly annoying: when the money was there, job creation should have been a priority. So, if our leaders couldn't do it, how are we to get the country up and running when we're now post-boom, borrowing money just to pay the wages? So a Yes vote sees the Irish people throwing a lifeline to Europe to save our sinking ship. Eamon Gilmore summed it up well, saying we were gritting our teeth while voting Yes.

Barber: I see you've been putting a bit of thought into your vote. I agree. We had no choice this time: it was sink or swim.

Customer: If only Castro wasn't so ill!

Weird cravings

5 October 2009

Customer: My girlfriend is pregnant, and I'm down in the 24-hour every other night buying stuff she's craving.

Barber: So what's the weirdest thing she's asked for?

Customer: Firelighters.

Tsunami warning in New Zealand

7 October 2009

A concerned parent told me this story while we were talking about the recent earthquake in Indonesia.

Customer: My son is in New Zealand at the moment, so I rang him when I heard about the earthquake and tsunami warning they had over there. I wanted to see if he was okay.

Barber: That must have been a worry. Was he all right?

Customer: Well, he was. He told me there was a warning on the radio to go to higher ground, and he said that, instead, everyone was heading to the beach with their surfboards!

Barber: No-one wanted to miss out on the ride of a lifetime!

Prison stories

9 October 2009

Customer: I was doing some work in Mountjoy Prison this week, and they have those disinfectant handwash gels everywhere because of the swine flu.

Barber: We have them here too. They're everywhere now.

Customer: Well, they were going through so many each day that the staff were confused. So they were keeping an eye, and they found that the prisoners were drinking them!

Barber: They have a lot of alcohol in the gel. It's probably like vodka if you mix it with orange juice. You must see some sights in there!

Customer: I do, but my favourite is the retro page-3 girls. Depending on how long the lads have been there, they could have pictures on their cell wall from the day they arrived. Someone serving time since the eighties would have pictures of Sam Fox or Linda Lusardi. It's a real blast seeing them again.

Barber: Wow, that was so long ago. Lusardi is in 'Emmerdale' now.

Customer: She's wearing more clothes now! Still a good-looking woman, though.

Shane MacGowan's tipple

10 October 2009

A barman from Eamonn Doran's (recently closed) told me this story:

Customer: Shane MacGowan was in Doran's a while ago. I think he's a friend of Dermot Doran. Anyway, he asked me for a pint of gin and lemon. 'Okay,' I said. 'Do you want lemon cordial or fizzy lemon?' 'No,' he says, 'a slice of lemon!'

Paddy Hitler

14 October 2009

Customer: Did you know Hitler's brother worked in the Shelbourne Hotel as a waiter?

Barber: Ah, that's not true.

Customer: It is true. He was a confidence trickster. He pretended to be a wealthy Austrian hotel-owner on a tour of Europe, and he ended up marrying a woman from Clondalkin. I'm telling you, look it up. See for yourself. His son was called Paddy Hitler.

Barber: Come on, now, I know you're having me on. Paddy Hitler?

Customer: You can say what you want, but that's a true story!

Short-sighted

15 October 2009

Customer: I had laser surgery on my eyes the other day!

Barber: I hear that works really well.

Customer: It's fantastic. It's like high definition. I was at a match the day after the surgery, and I could see the ball so clearly. Before it was just a blur!

Barber: I have that problem, but I never considered laser surgery. I can see perfectly close up, but I can't see anything clearly if it's far away.

Customer: You should try it. You won't believe how good it is. I decided to get my eyes done after I was waiting on a bus one day and I put my hand out to stop a Brennan's Bread van!

Remodelling

17 October 2009

Customer: I'd like a new style. Can you use a different bowl this time?

Barber: Smartarse!

On John O'Donoghue

25 October 2009

Customer: Did you see John O'Donoghue was flying up and down from Kerry to Dublin with his driver going earlier in the car so it would be there when he arrived? We were paying for an empty car going across the country. Spending like there was no tomorrow!

Barber: I heard someone on the radio say he was living on the other side of the wardrobe—in Narnia!

White overnight

27 October 2009

Customer: Take those hairs out of the ears there. Wait till you get to my age, they start growing everywhere except where they should. Did you know that?

Barber: Did I know what?

Customer: A good fright will turn the hair white overnight.

Barber: Ah, that's just an old wives' tale.

Customer: Well, you might say that, but I knew a woman years ago who had a terrible shock with the bangers in the letterbox at Halloween. She was watching 'The Late Late Show', and didn't some kids throw a couple through the door. She was the nervous type, you know. When she came home from the hospital her own family didn't know who she was! The hair had turned white overnight! The whole lot. And she had some head of hair. 'She won't go bald,' they used to say. Take those hairs off the neck there. That's better. Is it still raining? I'll run down to the pub and have a pint—stay in out of the rain.

Barber: Sounds like a good plan to me. Watch out for the bangers!

Fireworks

29 October 2009

Barber: It's quiet enough this year. Not so many fireworks going off.

Customer: Do you remember what it was like a couple of years ago? There were so many going off you could smell it in the air. It was like World War 3!

Clever sign

2 November 2009

Customer: I was in Portobello earlier. Do you know the antique shop there near the bridge?

Barber: Christy Bird's. I do indeed.

Customer: Well, they have a sign in the window that reads: 'Customers wanted, apply within.'

Holidays

3 November 2009

Customer: I went to Egypt for two weeks with my girlfriend. We're just back.

Barber: How did you get on?

Customer: It was great. The pyramids are incredible up close, but we had a bit of trouble one day. We were shopping and looking around in the city when a local lad grabbed my girlfriend and touched her up!

Barber: No way! Go on.

Customer: Yeah, the women over there are covered up, and my girlfriend was wearing shorts and a top. It's very hot, so you wouldn't want to be wearing too much, but this guy just grabbed her and groped her and ran away. She got a terrible shock, and a policeman came over and said they'd get the lad who did it. He asked us for the address of the hotel where we were staying and for our names. So we went back to the hotel and tried to forget about what happened. Later that evening the police came up to the room and told us they had got the guy. I thought this would be a relief, but they asked us if we wanted to press charges. I asked them what would happen, thinking he'd get a night in a cell or something that might teach him a lesson, but they said they'd cut off his hand!

Barber: My God!

Customer: I know, we were shocked. So we had a chat, and we didn't want they guy to lose his hand, so we didn't press charges in the end. It's a holiday we'll never forget!

Too big for his boots!

6 November 2009

Customer: I was on the bus on my way to work in town. It was raining, and the bus was full, with people standing in the corridor. Around the Coombe in Dublin a dwarf got on, and he had to stand up the front near the driver. A young girl in a school uniform who was sitting nearby got up and offered him her seat, but he was outraged by the gesture and gave her a lecture on political correctness—that he was a dwarf and not disabled—leaving her highly embarrassed. It was terrible. There was silence on the bus. A mature woman left her seat and made her way through the passengers to get off in the Liberties. Just as the bus stopped to let her off she looked down at the dwarf and said, loud enough for everyone to hear, 'See you—when you get home I hope Snow White knocks the shite out of you!' It was brilliant. Everyone just burst out laughing!

Cool T-shirt

7 November 2009

Haven't seen a lot of funny T-shirts lately, but a guy came in yesterday wearing one that read, 'Nice legs. What time do they open?'

It's safe to drink Bulmer's pear cider again!

10 November 2009

Since 1 November 2009 it's been safe to drink Bulmer's latest creation. There were lots of stories being heard in the refuge of the barber's chair concerning the laxative effects of the new brew.

Many a lad had confessed that he had about four or five pints on a night out and then all hell broke loose. Only those who were drinking the cider in the company of friends knew that it wasn't them, that it wasn't food poisoning and that it must have been the cider, as they all ran for the gents within minutes of each other. It reached a critical point when taxi-drivers began to complain. Because of the side effects of the cider, they were off the road for the night cleaning their cars! So now the new Bulmer's ads state that there's a new recipe. So don't be afraid: embrace the pear!

It's a dog's life

12 November 2009

Customer: I've been looking for a dog recently, and I was going to the animal shelter to pick one out, and after two visits I found a really nice labrador. So I gave them my details, because the people at the shelter come to your house to see if it's suitable for the dog. 'Fine,' I said. 'I'm free the next few days.' So they came and had a look and told me they wouldn't let the dog stay in the house. I was stunned! So when they were leaving I asked them, 'What about me?' 'What do you mean?' they said. 'Well, you say the house isn't fit for a dog to live in, but you're leaving me here, and you're going to get a better place for the dog!'

Dónal Óg

13 November 2009

There has been much controversy about Dónal Óg Cusack's coming out, and it didn't escape barber-shop conversations.

Customer: In a shop in the midlands I went to pay for my newspaper and saw that the old woman behind the counter had the paper open at the page with Dónal Óg's interview, so I asked her what she thought of Dónal announcing that he was gay. 'Ah,' she said, 'I think it's all in his head!'

Ireland v. France

20 November 2009

Not since Roy Keane left the Irish team in Saipan, not since Stephen Ireland refused to wear green has there been such anger and disillusionment, and now there's that awful feeling of injustice. All day every day since the World Cup qualifier on Wednesday every customer in the barber shop has been talking about the match!

It seems that the argument for a video ref in soccer is more valid than ever. Fans watching at home have more information than the ref, and they know what happened, with the advantage of slow-motion replays, whereas the ref is left to what he and the linesmen have seen in real time.

A customer who was at the match told me that the replay on the big screen in the Stade de France was shown from a different angle, making it difficult to spot the handball. It was fans at home watching who texted their friends at the game, telling them. Of course, there were others who had seen Thierry Henry's handball as it happened—Trapattoni being one. So we might be out, but maybe our protest will go down in history as the case for video refs in soccer.

It brought back memories of Maradona's 'Hand of God' that put England out of the World Cup. One of the papers ran the headline 'Hand of Frog!'

Limerick Christmas tree meets Shannon bridge

22 November 2009

What a weekend! Cork, Clare, Galway and Limerick all got the worst of the flooding. England is another story. A customer told me that after the quay wall collapsed in Cork there were people going through the city in kayaks. You read it here first: Cork is the new Venice.

Limerick had made a 100-foot green Christmas tree (from recycled metal), and it was being put in place in the River Shannon when it broke from its moorings and sailed away. It came to a sudden stop when it crashed into a bridge, causing it to be closed to traffic. Chaos, lads, chaos!

Moving statues

1 December 2009

We were talking about the moving statues that were in the news recently . . .

Customer: There was a statue of the Virgin Mary in Adare that never moved, so some joker put a sign on it saying, 'Out of order'!

Barber: That's brilliant.

Customer: It was in the paper and all. Trim those hairs in the ears there, will you? She's always trying to pull them out when I'm watching the telly.

The SUV brigade

2 December 2009

While we were talking about traffic jams in Dublin, the subject of SUVs and the traffic chaos around schools came up.

Customer: It's chock-a-block around the schools with the mothers dropping off their kids in SUVs. They just stop on the road and hold everyone up. It's madness!

Barber: I see it all the time. There's nowhere for them to park, though, but they shouldn't stop on the road.

Customer: Well, a woman held me up outside a school the other day, and then I'm down at the shopping centre, and there she is again, trying to park and holding everyone up again! The biggest SUV I've ever seen—huge it was. Shouldn't they do a separate driving test for people who drive them? I mean, they never do any 'off-roading.' They just use them to drop the kids to school and pick up the shopping!

Barber: It's a very expensive shopping trolley.

Customer: It's desperate, though. Maybe the recession will help a little, and they'll have to use more economical cars. Women, eh? Can't live with them, can't live without them!

Barber: You know the barber shop is probably the only place left where you can talk like this nowadays.

Customer: Or Portmarnock Golf Club!

Boss-napping: The new French trend
4 December 2009

When the lay-offs began throughout the world, a customer who works for an international company with offices in France told me this story:

Customer: There were some lay-offs in our branch, but when they tried to lay staff off in France it was a different story. The staff stuck together and locked the managers in their offices. They allowed the secretaries to get the managers a change of clothes and food each day. This went on for a few days until the decision to lay off staff was reversed. No charges were pressed, and everyone went back to work. They're doing it all the time over there now. Whenever there's redundancies announced, the managers are locked in. It's called boss-napping!

Barber: You don't mess with the French.

On the course

7 December 2009

Customer: I was out playing golf the other day. It was fairly late, and as it was so early in the week there was hardly anyone out on the course. So I was just taking it handy practising, and I teed off at the eighth hole. It's a really difficult hole to play, and I never got par—always a shot or two over—and this time, with no-one there with me to see, I got the ball on the green! I was delighted, but at the same time I was raging that no-one was there to witness it. So as long as I didn't mess up now, I could go under par.

As I was walking up to the green, which is on a rise that slopes down on the far side to the sea, I saw three lads waving to me from the next tee box. I thought for a minute they were congratulating me on my shot, but they kept waving, and I realise now they were trying to stop me walking up to the green. When I did I could see what the fuss was about: over the rise of the green, just out of my sight, until I got close enough, I saw a stark-naked woman with long dark hair sitting up, and from the look on her face and the moans she made, she was in the throes of passion. She was sitting on top of her partner, and their clothes were just thrown all around. My ball was lying only a few feet away from them.

The lads who were trying to get my attention were watching this and probably thought I'd disturb the romp, and they were trying to stop me going onto the green. But, like I said, I had never even got par on that hole, and I was determined that this time I would. So, despite the lovebirds, I walked up to the ball to putt it.

I could hear the couple going hard at it a few feet to my left, still in rapture. I don't even think they knew I was there.

I lined up the shot, took it and watched as the ball rolled down with the slope of the green and went into the hole. 'Yes!' I roared, and the couple froze. I looked at them with a beaming smile on my face, and she looked back at me in shock. I couldn't see your man. I picked my ball up and put my club away, and, as I was walking past the couple in my moment of glory, I said, 'Looks like we all got our hole today!'

The beer tray

8 December 2009

Customer: I was at the Pogues gig the other night. Man, it was brilliant! Shane MacGowan said that the beer tray is the best traditional Irish instrument!

Barber: The beer tray? How do you play a beer tray?

Customer: He hits it off his head. You know, like a drum.

Barber: Now why doesn't that surprise me!

Doomsday budget

9 December 2009

Customer: I thought I'd better get my hair cut today because I might not be able to afford it tomorrow.

Barber: Yeah, the media are making it out that the whole country will be like Limerick in *Angela's Ashes*.

Customer: And Gormley? What's he doing? Looking for over a hundred grand to count frogs?

Barber: I heard that Enda Kenny said Gormley was hopping mad. You know they're calling them the Light Greens now?

Customer: Why don't we just hand the country back to the English? Then we wouldn't have to go up North to buy drink, and they might build a few schools too.

Barber: Or the French . . .

Customer: Oh, no, not after Henry's handball. No, we should just march the Government down to Dublin Castle—I wouldn't let those lads run the Tayto factory, by the way—a few of the bankers and bishops too, and have a firing squad waiting. The police would be on our side, after the pension contribution fiasco. Then we could get rid of NAMA and start again—just like rewinding the clock back to 1922.

Barber: That would fix it. We might get it right this time. Independence isn't easy!

Monk hijacks plane!

10 December 2009

This story came up recently in the shop, and no-one believed it except for the customer whose hair I was doing and who brought it up in the first place. The third 'secret' of Fátima was a mystery. I remember hearing that it foretold the end of the world and the events that would unfold as that time approached. But this knowledge was only known to the Pope. To most it wasn't important, but it preoccupied some, and they became known as Fátima fanatics. Now, the third secret was published a few years ago, and it didn't seem as dramatic as we had been led to believe. But, during the years when it was unknown, it drove a particular monk to do something reckless—on an Aer Lingus flight! I heard the story shortly after it happened from a customer who worked for the airline. The story went something like this . . .

Barber (as the customer sat in the chair): Hi, how are you?

Customer: I've just had a hectic week!

Barber: Why? What happened?

Customer: We had a plane hijacked that was going to England but ended up in Paris.

Barber: My God. Who did that?

Customer: Believe it or not, it was a monk, and he threatened to set fire to himself and blow up the plane!

Barber: That's mad. A monk! Was anyone hurt?

Customer: No, thank heaven. There were 113 people on board. It was one of our planes, so we had to go over to sort it out.

Barber: So what were his demands?

Customer: That's the strangest thing about his hijacking: he wanted to know the third secret of Fátima!

There was silence for a moment as I looked at him in the mirror in disbelief.

Barber: And did the Vatican tell him? [I asked, hoping they did, and that now he was going to tell me!]

Customer: No, the plane was stormed by French Special Forces at Le Touquet, and they arrested him and took him away.

Barber: That's some story!

Gay football
12 December 2009

Customer: Did you hear about the gay football team in Tallaght?

Barber: No, are you serious?

Customer: Yeah, and guess what the team is called.

Barber: I really have no idea.

Customer: Men United!

Hardcore GAA fan
13 December 2009

Barber: Will you be watching the rugby tomorrow?

Customer: Jaysus, no, I don't watch that kiss-chasing!

Tiger's not out of the woods yet
14 December 2009

Customer: What is it with that Tiger Woods story that everyone is so obsessed with?

Barber: It certainly has everyone talking, all right. Are you a fan?

Customer: No, I'm not interested in golf at all, but that cocktail waitress he was with—man, she is something! In my estimation he's gone from zero to hero now!

American tourists in Dublin
15 December 2009

A couple of American tourists in Dublin ask a local person, 'Excuse me, is that Christ's Church over there?' The Dubliner says, 'Well, as far as I know, love, they're all his!'

That bank in Tallaght

16 December 2009

A story from a few months ago that made the headlines: A certain bank claimed that it knew nothing of the party held by the Institute of Technology, Tallaght, in a local bar, where erotic dancers were booked for a night. The bank was allegedly using it to promote student accounts. (You got a free ticket when you opened an account.)

Customer: I'm studying in the Tallaght Institute.

Barber: Oh, yeah. Did you know about that erotic dance night?

Customer: That was gas. Everyone was talking about it.

Barber: And did the bank know?

Customer: Sure they did! The students were going in asking if they could open a stripper account!

Christmas in Siberia

17 December 2009

I was feeling a bit down with the recession and the weather and with the 'doomsday budget' approaching, but my next customer was about to change my outlook.

Barber: Hi, what will we do today?

Customer: Cut it shorter than usual. I'll be away for a few weeks for Christmas and the New Year.

Barber: No problem. Where are you off to?

Customer: Siberia.

Barber: Siberia! it must be extremely cold over there right now.

Customer: Yep, up to minus thirty. My wife is from there.

Barber: And here I was feeling sorry for myself because it won't stop raining here. You wouldn't be able to go out in temperatures that low, would you?

Customer: Well, my wife said we couldn't go ice-skating if it gets below minus fifteen. It's dangerous: last year a bus broke down travelling between two villages, and when the rescue party arrived everyone on the bus was dead.

Barber: I guess I've little reason to complain.

Customer: The economy is pretty bad too. It's like going back in time when you arrive over there—like the sixties or seventies was here.

Barber: Well, I hope you enjoy Christmas over there.

Customer: Don't worry about me. I'll be out ice-skating!

My, how things have changed!

18 December 2009

Customer: We used to shop in New York; now we go to Newry!

Clothes and hair in the recession

19 December 2009

Customer (who works in the clothes trade): How's business these days?

Barber: It's not as good as it was over the last few years, but there are a lot of hairdressers' and barber shops that are very quiet. It depends on the location, really.

Anyone in an industrial estate is very quiet. A lot of beauty salons are going to the wall. How are you finding it?

Customer: Very quiet. It's very worrying.

Barber: On the radio they were talking to Louis Copeland, and he said people in clothes and hair trades always do well in a recession because everyone wants to look their best. In the boom years people dressed down, but in the recession they dress up.

Customer: Well, the eighties were like that. I worked through it, and it was very busy, but they were all dressing up for interviews. Everyone was on the dole and doing interviews all the time.

Barber: I remember those days, and that's true. Most people getting a haircut would be going for an interview!

Customer: So that's the difference, you see: no-one is doing interviews now!

Shopping online

24 December 2009

'Twas the day before Christmas
. . . and the barber shop was stirring . . .

Customer: Did you get all your Christmas shopping done yet?

Barber: I did. I've been doing it online for the last few years. I'm not really into shopping: if I go into town I like to just ramble round and maybe have lunch or go for a coffee. I have to say, though, I find there's less and less choice in the shops if you're looking for something different. You know, most shops seem to be going more and more mainstream with their stock. Even in the bookshops there are certain sections that just disappeared in the last few years.

Customer: You're looking for more specialist items then, yeah?

Barber: I am, and I always thought that when the web got going here shops would become more specialised, especially the smaller ones, in order to survive, but it hasn't happened. Maybe the population is too small, as the specialist market would be smaller again. Do you shop online yourself?

Customer: I do. I really enjoy it, and then you get the package in the post. I'm like a kid opening it! Did you ever buy clothes online?

Barber: No, I haven't. I'm put off by the thought of getting something and having to send it back if it's too small or doesn't fit right.

Customer: You should. I do. If you see something you like, try it on in a shop, get the right size and then order it online. Simple. Lots of people are doing it!

Barber: I never thought of that, but it must piss off the retailers. It's funny too, you know, all the people who travel to Newry get grilled in the media, and all of us who buy most of our stuff online are left alone, like we are the unseen, unheard unpatriots!

Customer: Even when you tell people who are against Newry shopping that you shop online they don't react to it. Is there an underlying attitude problem there? Like, online shopping is fine, but the others are killing the Southern retail market? 'Cause we are spending our cash outside the country too!

Barber: You know, that's a very good point!

New Year's Eve in Dublin

2 January 2010

Customer: I was in town on New Year's, and none of us realised it had been snowing outside. I guess we were too busy ringing in the new year. Anyway, when we came outside to get a taxi it was a whiteout—snow everywhere. We tried for a while, but there was no way to get a taxi, and we started walking. There were drunken people everywhere, slipping and sliding, and some fell badly. On the way up through Rathmines there was blood splattered on the footpaths where people had slipped, and we guessed they hit their heads—it was that bad! We passed small groups all gathered round helping people who had fallen, too wasted to get back up. There must have been some sore heads on New Year's Day!

Barber: A doctor told me earlier he was working in A&E, and he said they were really busy with injuries from people falling on the ice. It must have been chaotic!

Customer: Well, I won't be going into town for New Year's next year. I'm fed up having to walk home!

More New Year's disasters

3 January 2010

Customer: Man, it was hellish getting home from town on New Year's. The taxis didn't even come into town. There were girls in high heels pissed and trying to walk in the snow. They were falling everywhere, and it wasn't like they could take off their heels, or they'd have ended up with frostbite!

Barber: I've heard so many stories about it. One lad told me he couldn't walk up Portobello Bridge, and he saw someone take off their socks and put them over their shoes to get a grip on the snow, so he did the same and got over the bridge!

Christmas Eve on Grafton Street

4 January 2010

Customer: I was going up Grafton Street on Christmas Eve, and, outside Captain America's, Bono, Damien Rice and Glen Hansard were busking. There was a huge crowd around them, but you could get close enough to see them. It was a real surprise. It's on Youtube, but the quality isn't great!

Serious lack of proper weather reports

5 January 2010

Customer: I can't believe there's no information on the radio or TV about the weather. I'm driving to Galway for New Year's later, and I don't know what the roads are like, or if I'll even get there.

(Because of heavy snowfall and forecasts of temperatures anywhere between minus seven and minus thirteen, depending on which radio station you listen to.)

Barber: You know, when Henry played the handball, that's all they talked about on the radio and TV for three days, when in the west, Carlow and Wexford—counties not even reported—they had some of the worst flooding in living memory!

Customer: Well, anyone I know who travelled to

Galway that week couldn't get past Ballinasloe. It was flooded and there were no reports on the main stations.

Barber: Did you try looking online for info?

Customer: Yeah, I did. I found a web site that had a forecast that read, 'Weather likely to be wintry in nature!'

Barber: We just don't have enough nerds in this country. If we did, all that information would be there!

We don't do extremes!

6 January 2010

Customer: The schools aren't open, some roads are gritted and some aren't, the forecast is consistently wrong—man, we don't do extremes in Ireland, whether it's weather or the economy.

Barber: I saw a bumper sticker on a car recently that said, 'Please send us another Tiger—we'll look after this one!'

New car dealerships in Ireland

7 January 2010

Customer: My daughter went into the bank to get a loan for a car, and they asked her what sort of car she was looking for, so she said a Mini. She came home and told me they had a few Minis that she looked at. She picked the one she liked, and the bank gave her the loan. It was repossessed. They have so many now—some only a year or two old, low mileage—and she got a great deal!

Barber: I heard the insurance companies are doing something similar: if you write a car off they offer you a replacement—same model, same year. Not so good for the lads burning a car out in order to get the cash: they go down, expecting to get a cheque, and they get a replacement!

Customer: I wonder if the banks are selling off property too. I might look into that—see if I can pick up a cheap villa in Portugal.

Global warming

8 January 2010

Customer: I don't really buy the whole global warming story. I did hear an interesting thing, though, about the idea that the Earth is heating up and that it heats up like any other organism, to burn off a disease—and in this case we're the disease!

Barber: That's weird. But you know the TV series 'Lost'? The idea behind that is that there's a reversal of the poles, and the ice caps melt, and basically everything is reversed: that's why you have polar bears on a tropical island. See, in the future when the reversal happens you would—or could—have a tropical Ireland, and the Spanish would come here on holiday, making Bray a very good idea for future investment— just to keep it in mind. So the polar reversal or magnetic changeover is a theory that some scientists believe is cyclical. It makes you think, you know, maybe the Vikings invaded us all those years ago to take over our banana plantations. There was a desert in Antrim a long way back. That's true—saw it on TV. Anyway, true or not, global warming is giving us a healthy awareness of the Earth and of looking after it in the future!

Hill-surfing

10 January 2010

This happened yesterday. We were very quiet in the morning because of the whiteout—snow everywhere. Even the staff from the local petrol station told us their pumps were frozen and that diesel was freezing in cars. It was the coldest I remember. Nice and fresh, though, when the sun came out . . .

Customer: I just saw some lads go past the window with surfboards!

Barber: Yeah, a few went by earlier. They're going down to the hill. There were literally about eighty people down there last night sledging or going down the hill on plastic bags, but today the surfboards came out. Gas!

Technology

12 January 2010

Customer: My first proper PC had a 1.4 gig hard drive—a Compaq, I think. Now my phone has 8 gigs, which was only in the last ten years!

Barber: It's amazing how fast technology is moving. I heard you can use an early Windows operating system on a mobile like that.

Customer: Even iPods have huge memory. Imagine someone told you ten or fifteen years ago that you could store your entire music collection on something smaller than a cigarette packet. You wouldn't have believed it.

Driving in snow

19 January 2010

We had Polish people laughing at our attempts to drive
in snow and ice, but here's a new perspective on
driving in bad conditions:

Customer: I used to live in LA, and they don't get rain
there very often—maybe once or twice a year—but
sometimes they get rain that's similar to heavy rain here
in Ireland. But that's rare—as rare as snow is here.
When they get rain like that there are crashes
everywhere, and people abandon their cars on the
motorway! We used to laugh at the chaos, just like the
Poles are laughing at us driving in snow. It's just
whatever you're used to.

Barber: Or not used to!

Car park warning

20 January 2010

Recently I've been hearing stories told by those who
had, without realising it, parked in someone's space.
The best of which was:

Customer: I parked in someone's private space in a car
park in town without realising, and when I came back
my wipers were broken off the windscreen and shoved
up my exhaust!

Barber: I still can't believe someone would be so angry
that they'd do that! I heard a few similar stories. It
seems it was a trend for a while.

Frozen window-washers

21 January 2010

Customer: Still snowing, eh? The window-washers on my car are freezing up, and I couldn't clear the windscreen. Very dangerous, that, especially now with all the slush on the motorways. The trucks spray your windscreen with slush and dirt.

Barber: Tell me about it! The trucks are doing almost a hundred kilometres per hour on the motorways, and, when they go past, your windscreen is covered in grime and slush in seconds. One lad told me he did fifty miles before his washers would work.

Customer: Well, I went into about four garages on the way home the other night to get a windscreen-washer liquid that had antifreeze in it, and everywhere was sold out, so I remembered a cheap bottle of vodka I got for Christmas. I'd never have opened it, so I filled the windscreen-washer with it. And guess what! It works!

Iris Robinson and Ikea

23 January 2010

Customer: What do Iris Robinson and Ikea have in common?

Barber: No idea.

Customer: One dodgy screw and the whole cabinet falls apart!

Things may be getting better!

24 January 2010

The car parks are filling up. People are beginning to spend again. Phones are ringing in offices. Payments are arriving in businesses without the accounts department having to ring and remind or demand. Delivery drivers are working late. Hey, I even had to oil my clippers a few times today. Since the snow cleared, people are spending again. Was it all a confidence thing? Let's hope!

No they're not!

25 January 2010

A lot of customers were talking about the way things had turned around, but it was only for a short while. It turns out that the mini-boom was the result of everyone getting paid after Christmas for the first time in six weeks. This, added to the effect of being snowed in for days, meant that everyone went out and spent for a few days. Back to the recession . . .

BMWs don't do snow!

26 January 2010

Customer: I've had to leave the BMW at home. I'm driving the wife's car instead: the Beemer is hopeless in this weather.

Barber: Yeah, Mercs too. There are lots of them sitting in driveways, covered in snow, that haven't been driven since New Year's.

Customer: It's mad paying forty grand plus for a car and

then finding it can't hold its own in the snow. It's the rear-wheel drive: no weight over the wheels.

Barber: I used to have a Volkswagen Beetle, and there was a similar problem with the front, so people put a sack of potatoes or a concrete block in the boot. I'd imagine that would work for a rear-wheel drive car!

Customer: Would you feck off with your sack of potatoes!

Doomsday radio

27 January 2010

Customer: I've taken Newstalk and RTE1 off the presets on my radio. I can't listen to that doomsday journalism any more.

Barber: I can't count the number of people who said they've stopped listening to those stations. The radio would have you feeling suicidal.

Rain sensors on cars

28 January 2010

We were talking about rain sensors on cars when a customer told us:

Customer: Yeah, they're good, but I had a new Mercedes there two years ago, and my wife took it to the garage and went through a car wash. She didn't know there was a rain sensor, and the wipers were ruined. They came on full when the water was spraying on the windscreen. Then the brushes started, and they were mangled!

Extreme sports

29 January 2010

Customer: I was on holiday in Rio and did some paragliding with friends who do it regularly. We went up the mountain, and near the top we met some people coming back down saying there was a storm coming in. We saw nothing only blue sky, so, as we were almost at the top, we decided to jump. There were four of us, and we were all in the air in minutes out over the sea. It was beautiful, but then dark clouds appeared in the sky. I knew they were dangerous, so I started descending to lose some height. One of the lads was up quite high still, and the cloud started to suck him up.

Barber: How do you mean, 'it sucked him up'?

Customer: The storm clouds you get in tropical countries are like a vacuum, and they suck air up through them. The clouds trap all the moisture in the air. They suck through, and the moisture freezes, and later it'll fall as hailstones. So my mate was being pulled up towards the cloud. He would've died if he went into it, because the hailstones inside are like rocks, and they're in the cloud flying around—you'd be battered to death. So he cut his canopy straps and came flying past me and on down into the sea. He survived, but it was as close as you'd ever want to come!

Car loan, anyone?

31 January 2010

A customer in the second-hand car trade told me today that they had a busy week—the busiest Saturday in ten years, to quote him exactly. He said the banks were beginning to give out car loans again!

Still no bank help for small businesses

1 February 2010

Customer: I tried to get a bank loan of €100,000 to expand my business. The company is doing well through the recession, and I need to grow the business. But my application was turned down by the bank! A few weeks later I applied for a loan for a car—an expensive car. I asked for €120,000, and the bank approved the loan!

A lift home from the pub, Aran Island-style!

2 February 2010

Customer: I was in the Aran Islands recently on a break, and one night in a pub we asked the barman if we could get a taxi home. He called out to a man sitting at the back of the pub: 'These people are looking for a lift.' 'No problem,' the man said. 'I'll be ready in a few minutes.' He went back to talking to some friends. Anyway, we finished our drinks and went outside, but there was no car in the street. Puzzled, I asked the driver, who was just coming out the door, where the car was. He had a big grin on his face as he walked round by the side of the pub! 'Here she is,' he said loudly as he reappeared with a horse and cart. We got into the cart, and he told us there was a blanket in the back that we could throw over our legs if we were cold!

An unexpected reply . . .

3 February 2010

Barber: I haven't seen you for a while. Your hair has gotten very long.

Customer: Ah, I had a rough few weeks there. My brother committed suicide.

Barber: God, I'm really sorry to hear that.

Customer: No need: it was the best thing he ever did.

The head on that!

4 February 2010

A customer came into the shop with the longest matted curly hair I've ever seen, when another customer, who was waiting, shouted out, 'Are you getting that mop cut or are you just getting an estimate?'

Cheap hotels

10 February 2010

Barber: The prices that hotels are offering are great: it's cheaper to stay in town now than to get a taxi home if you live outside Dublin.

Customer: I've seen them. Sure at those prices we should rent our houses out and move into a hotel!

George Lee

12 February 2010

Customer: Ah, I think George was naïve to think that his ideas would be listened to.

Barber: Did you hear the rumours that he left because the expenses cut was coming? And some think he bailed to get Charlie Bird's job in Washington!

Customer: Well, whatever the reason, I imagine he thought he was welcomed into the Fine Gael party because he had a rare perspective. He had ideas, and they were relevant.

Barber: So why didn't they fast-track his top-ten list to the boardroom meetings? Why else would they bring him on board?

Customer: Unfortunately, Fine Gael didn't see it like that. A celebrity like George brings a lot of kudos to the party. I think that's all they wanted from him. So I'm hoping George Lee will publish some of his ideas so we can see what went into Enda's wastepaper basket—if they even got that far. That would be a real embarrassment for Fine Gael if there were good ideas in there.

Barber: And I thought we were moving forward for a moment . . .

Cowlicks

16 February 2010

Barber: Wow, this is a challenge!

Customer: Tell me about it! I've got so many cowlicks my mother says I was born in a cow shed!

Willie O'Dea (on his resignation)

19 February 2010

Customer: Did you see O'Dea on the news last night?

Barber: No, I missed that. What was he saying?

Customer: It was very funny. The reporters met him outside on the street, and he started off saying he wasn't pushed, that he had resigned of his own free will. So the reporters were taunting him a little to get a reaction out of him, and one asked him again if Cowen had asked him to leave, and he responded by saying, 'No, as I said, I decided for the good of the country that I would step down, otherwise it could have brought the Government down, and we can't have that right now, so I did it in the best interests of the country!' Hilarious. But the best bit was at the end when a reporter asked him if he thought he had been unfairly treated by the party, and he said, off the top of his head, 'Of course I do. I stood by other party members when they were in trouble, and they did much worse things than I did.'

Barber: I can't believe he said that. So he's telling us he was loyal even to the point of protecting the guilty. Good job he's gone, then.

Customer: He was gas, though. I remember a friend of mine went to a fancy-dress party with a pair of the Marx Brothers' glasses, with the fake nose and moustache. Do you remember them?

Barber: I do. They sell them in joke shops. I haven't seen them for a while, though.

Customer: They're the ones. Well, he wore them, and he had a toy shotgun, and he went as Willie O'Dea.

He looked just like him! It was just after the picture of him in the front page of the paper looking down the barrel of a rifle!

Porsche tests new models in Mayo and Sligo

2 March 2010

Customer: I saw a blacked-out, taped-up Porsche 997 and a Boxster outside a pub in Mayo. They were disguised, so you couldn't see the new shape. It was a few years ago now, but it's something I won't forget. It was months before the cars went on sale. The drivers were obviously having some lunch in the pub—it was in the middle of nowhere!

Barber: I heard Toyota does that too to set up the suspension. Funny the things you happen upon in this country!

Home bleaching

3 March 2010

Customer: I bleached my hair at home and left it on too long, and I hate it. It's so white and curly—it's like Super Noodles.

Barber: It really is!

The natives are restless

4 March 2010

Customer: It's incitement to revolution, it is! Bertie should be keeping his head down. Unheard and unseen, I tell you! He's got no shame. Do you remember what he said to the economists who warned about the bubble bursting? 'I don't know how people who engage in that don't commit suicide,' he said. Haughey was right when he said Bertie was the most cunning of all.

Barber: He did say that. And, of all people, Charlie would have known.

Customer: Did you see his daughter in the weekend supplement full-page spread, lying across a chaise longue in a ball gown or something? Looks like it was taken in window of the Shelbourne Hotel. Had no-one in the paper the sense to stop that story in a recession? We need to get the French over and bring a guillotine or two over with them so we can revolt. They'll show us what to do! We'll take Enda Kenny out too; no-one will vote for Fine Gael until they get him out. They need to put Richard Bruton in there instead. Kenny is a clown.

Barber: A lot of people have said that they'd vote for Fianna Fáil again rather than have Enda Kenny as Taoiseach. Maybe they'll leave Kenny in so they won't win and won't have to clean up the mess.

Watered-down petrol!

6 March 2010

Customer: I can't believe the price of petrol lately. Last year, when it started going up, everyone was talking about it, but this year I haven't heard anyone mention it on the radio or on TV.

Barber: I know, it's €1.32 in some places now.

Customer: It's like they're watering it down. A full tank doesn't last at all.

Barber: A customer told me the filling stations that advertise that they use an additive that cleans your engine are actually diluting the fuel with the additive, as it's cheaper and means they get more profit!

Customer: Well, I can believe it.

Getting mortgages . . .

7 March 2010

I've been hearing from customers how difficult it's been to get a mortgage. It's nigh on impossible, it seems, since the global downturn, and then I heard this . . .

Customer: I work in construction, and the only clients we've had in the last few months for extensions or new house builds that are getting mortgages all had one thing in common: they all work in the bank!

Barber: That would suggest that their bank jobs are secure?

Customer: God only knows, but one client, who had a well-paid, secure job for twenty-six years, couldn't get the loan he needed to extend his house.

Wheelie bins

13 March 2009

Customer: Why does the same truck pick up the brown and black bins?

Cloning around
14 May 2009

Customer: You must end up with lots of hair clippings at the end of the day. Is there anything you can do with them?

Barber: Well, not really. The cuttings are too short to be used for wigs.

Customer: You could use the hair to clone customers.

Barber: That's something that never crossed my mind, strangely enough.

Customer: You could, you know. Not all of them, mind you—just the good ones.

How to get the guards in a hurry!
16 March 2010

Customer: I was at home the other night. It was late, and I saw two people outside walking or sneaking across the garden. I said nothing to my wife. I didn't want to frighten her. I went out of the room where we were watching TV and rang the guards. I told them that there were two lads outside in the garden, that we were alone in the house and that we live in a detached house in the country. The guard on the phone told me they were too busy to call out. They told me that I should bolt the door and that they'd come out when they had time. I took their advice and bolted the door.

I looked out a window and saw that the two strangers were still snooping around, so I decided to ring the guards again, and, pretending I was out of breath and frightened, I told them that I had been on earlier—I had given my name and address before—that

I had shot at the two trespassers and that I thought I'd hit one of them! Within minutes there were two garda cars and an ambulance, and there was a helicopter hovering above with a searchlight. They got the two lads, who got some shock, I'll tell you. They must have thought they were casing a celebrity's home. So the guards came up to me, and one of them said, 'I thought you said you'd shot one of them.' And I said, 'I thought you said you were busy!'

Lock-hards

18 March 2010

Victims of the Celtic Tiger, the lock-hards are a part of Dublin culture that has become extinct in recent years. I was reminded of them the other day by a customer who told me this story:

Customer: I was parking my car at St Stephen's Green when a lock-hard came over and started shouting his catchphrase, 'Lock hard!' He was shouting through the window. Anyway, I ignored him, parked and got out. I had my dog and, as I was only stopping for ten minutes or so, left it in the car. 'I'll keep an eye on the car for you,' the lock-hard said, holding out his hand for a tip. Well, I never tipped those guys—it only encouraged them. So I said, 'No, thanks, the car will be okay.' 'Are you sure?' he says, with a sarcastic smile. 'Of course it will be. I have my dog in the back,' I replied. I begin to walk off, and the lock-hard shouts, 'Can he put out a fire?' He earned his tip!

Seánie Fitzpatrick
19 March 2010

Customer 1: It's a great day today: the weather is good, and Seánie spent the night in a cell.

Barber: Everyone's talking about it. I can't imagine he got much sleep.

Customer 2 (in the next chair): I don't think there are many bank managers in the country who slept last night!

Colder than you think!
24 March 2010

After being surprised by reports of terrible weather in Wellington, Australia, for the Irish rugby match, I was told by a customer, 'Sure there's penguins on the beaches in Wellington. That's how cold it gets over there.'

You're not in the colonies now!
25 March 2010

An American tourist staying at the Sheen Falls in Co. Kerry rings the reception desk late one night complaining that he can't sleep and could they turn off the waterfall!

Shop talk
25 March 2010

Barber 1: Did you put the kettle on? I asked you ages ago.

Barber 2: I tried, but it didn't fit.

Pubs open on Good Friday in Limerick

26 March 2010

The news announcing that the pubs in Limerick would be open on Good Friday came on the radio in the shop.

Customer (from Limerick): Did you hear that? He's done it: the pubs will be open on Good Friday!

Barber: How did he manage that? Even the Government was against it.

Customer: I don't know, but Kiely [the Mayor of Limerick] will be voted in for the rest of his life!

Spring forward, fall back

27 March 2010

Barber: You know, the clocks change tonight, but I can never remember if they go forward or back an hour.

American customer: Well, in the States we have a saying: 'Spring forward, fall back.' That way you won't forget. Good, eh?

Barber: Hey, that's really clever. And we always thought yous Yanks were thick!

Irish road signs—it's a genetic thing . . .

28 March 2010

Customer: Don't talk to me about the road signs in this country! My God, how tourists get around this country is beyond me!

Barber: Especially when you leave the airport: if you can find the M50, every exit on it is signposted as an exit to the city centre. I don't get that.

Customer: And why are the signs after the slip roads rather than before? I've seen people reverse on the M50 to get back to the off ramp, which is madness, anyway!

Barber: One of the older customers who comes in told me there's a theory that the signage thing goes back a long way in our genes. He said that, for years, people were turning sign posts around to point in the wrong direction so that British soldiers would get lost going out across the country! He said that in some places you can still see evidence of this. I remember seeing signposts where I live turned to face the wrong direction, so it could well be a genetic hand-down from our forefathers.

Customer: He could have something there, all right. So now when we have to do the job properly we are unable to! We're experts in misdirection.

McPorridge

29 March 2010

Customer: Great the way everyone is so health-conscious these days: they serve porridge in McDonald's now.

Barber: Porridge? Are you serious? I can't imagine that.

Customer: Oh, yeah, McPorridge, I think it's called. I suppose they have to move with the times.

Barber: That's very funny. It just sounds all wrong. Do they do a McPorridge meal?

A blonde moment!

2 April 2010

This story has been round the block. I even met the woman involved—or at least she claimed to be—but she never told me this had all ended up in court! A customer who was involved in the case brought it all back to me today . . .

Customer: I was involved in a case years ago in which a judge had gone to a hairdresser to get his hair cut. Afterwards he was sitting in the chair with a gown on, and he was waiting for someone to come over and blow-dry his hair. A pretty young woman came over to him and, after introducing herself, began drying his hair. The judge was fiddling round under the gown for a moment. Then, to the hairdresser's surprise, the old man began to jerk the gown up and down around his lap. She looked on in horror, watching as this old guy was for all the world jerking off under the gown! As she watched in disbelief, the gown kept moving up and down in a rhythm. Suddenly she whacked him across the back of the head really hard with her hairdrier! 'You dirty bastard!' she screamed. Everyone in the shop turned to see what all the commotion was about. Then the manager came over. 'What the hell are you doing?' he asks. The hairdresser rips the gown off the customer and turns his chair round for all to see. But it wasn't what she expected: underneath the gown, the dazed and confused judge had been innocently polishing his glasses on his lap!

He won his case.

Noisy kid in the barber shop

4 April 2010

There was a three-year-old boy in the shop, and his mother was telling him that he was a big boy and that he had to have his hair cut. He was having none of it, so he started screaming crying—and I mean *screaming*. The lad whose hair I was doing turned round to the mother with a grin and said, 'How much does he charge to haunt a house?'

We all burst out laughing.

The Dáil bar

5 April 2010

Customer: I was in the Dáil bar recently, and it's like a snapshot of the past. The men and women sit separately: the men at the bar, mostly, and the women around in groups, like a country dance-hall in the sixties. The men at the bar were throwing back the pints before their lunch, and they were telling sexist and racist jokes. Then the food was served like a carvery lunch—real old style, lots of gravy and mash. Then, when they finished knocking back the pints, they went in to vote!

Barber: I have to say I'm not at all surprised.

Vending machine in Somerset

7 April 2010

Customer: I was on a stag party in Somerset recently, and guess what they sell in the vending machines in the gent's toilets!

Barber: No idea. What?

Customer: Viagra, condoms and inflatable sheep. Seriously! I'm not joking!

Barber: That's like a one-man show.

3D football

8 April 2010

Customer: Ah, I hear it's not great for football unless they have close-ups. You'd need more cameras to get more shots of the ball coming towards the screen, which leads me to an idea a friend of mine had for a laugh. He said, 'Bring a football to the pub, and then at some stage throw it into the crowd watching the match!'

The Planning Department

9 April 2010

Customer: I have a friend who lives in the Waterways in Sallins, Co. Kildare, and, if you remember, they were totally flooded back in November. The cars were almost floating in the car park! He told me a local person had mentioned that the place used to flood regularly in the past and that they called it the swamp. It was a pitch-and-putt course, and it would flood so badly that you could see the flags but not the flagpoles! How they ever got planning in flood plains is beyond me. My friend said the management company had gone bust in the recession, so I said he should contact the builder, and he told me they'd gone out of business too!

Barber: Their apartments and houses are worthless now, as they can't get insurance. Nothing has been done, so the chances are they'll flood again in the future. It really is a terrible situation. A customer told me recently that the Planning Department didn't have many inspectors going round the new estates being built to check that the work was being done properly, and that, as a result, the quality of the work suffered in some developments. But the wastewater from washing machines and dishwashers is going straight into the domestic wastewater pipe, which, in a lot of cases, ends up in local rivers and streams. And, according to this particular customer who tests the river water, it's killing a lot of the ecology. No more tadpoles in the rivers and God knows what else!

Customer: There had to have been a lot of brown envelopes going round, that's all I can say.

Potholes

11 April 2010

Customer: I hit a pothole last week. After the snow the roads have been in a terrible state. Anyway, it nearly took the wheel off my car: it damaged the rim and blew out the tyre. I was so angry! A friend of mine knew a lad in the council, and he told me to go up and ask for him, as he could compensate me for the damage. So it took a phone call and I was up at the council offices waiting for this lad. He was nice enough, and he asked me about the damage. Then he asked me where the pothole was. I told him, and he says, 'Ah, that's not our hole!'

Barber: That's brilliant. So whose hole was it?

Customer: He said that the gas company had been digging up that road last and that the council wasn't responsible for it once they'd been there. I gave up after that.

Why we don't like fish!

13 April 2010

Customer: Do you know why we don't eat much fish in Ireland? I mean to say, for an island nation we have an abundance of fish, but people don't care for it.

Barber: I've often wondered why. The French, Spanish and Greek people all love their fish: they even have fishing rights in our waters, thanks to the Government, which gave our fishing grounds to Europe.

Customer: Well, it being Good Friday yesterday, I remember travelling as a young lad down to hotels in the midlands, and the church made it a sin to eat meat, so we were more or less told to eat fish on Fridays—not just Good Friday. But in the midlands they didn't have fish in the hotels, as it wasn't possible to transport from the coast to the country and keep it fresh, so they'd offer you two boiled eggs and toast with a pot of tea! That's the reason we don't eat fish here: it was seen as penance food.

Checkpoint Charlie!

14 April 2010

A customer told me this story many years ago, and it's supposed to be true.

A business man called Charlie drove home from the pub very drunk late one night and got stopped by the guards at a checkpoint. There was a garda car by the footpath, and he parked behind it. They realised he was hammered and asked him to get out of the car. It was a while before he could get standing on the road beside them, and he was swaying gently from side to side.

The guards were about to breathalyse him when a car came speeding round the corner, left the road and crashed into the ditch! The two guards ran to the crash, leaving the drunken man alone. Charlie decided to make a break for it and impulsively jumped into the car and drove home as fast as he could. He told his wife that he had been stopped and that if anyone happened to call she was to say that he'd been in all night. Next morning the doorbell rang. The man's wife opened the door to two guards.

'Is your husband here?' they asked her.

'Yes, he is. Why, is there something wrong?' she asked innocently.

'Well, we think he drove off from a garda checkpoint late last night.'

'Oh, no! It couldn't have been him. He was here last night with me.'

'I see,' the guard said. 'Could we speak to him?'

'Sure, hold on.—Charlie?'

A few minutes later the businessman came down, fresh from the shower.

'Good morning,' he said. 'How can I help you?'

'Good morning. We believe you drove away from a checkpoint in Stillorgan last night.'

'Ah, now, that couldn't have been me. I had a quiet night in last night.'

'Well, would you mind if we took a look at your car?'

'Sure, that's no problem. It's in the garage. I'll just get the keys.'

So they walked over to the garage, and, calmly and confidently, Charlie turns the key and pulls up the garage door. To his absolute horror, the car in the garage is a garda car!

'How did you think we found out where you lived?' the guards asked him. 'You left your car at the checkpoint, so we ran your number-plate.'

Motorways in Ireland

15 April 2010

Customer: Everyone is off today, it being Good Friday, and I came up the motorway. By the way, it's a beautiful day in Cork—the sun is shining. Anyway, I come up a lot, but on bank holidays there's less traffic—but it's nuts! Everyone is doing whatever speed they want in whatever lane they want. On a working day the traffic is much more streamlined. There was a crash on the N7, and I thought, 'No wonder!' It's a free-for-all.

Barber: I'm always asking people what lanes they use on the motorway, and very few people know. I only found out recently that you stay in the inside lane and that the other two are only for overtaking; but it hasn't even been in the Rules of the Road till last year! My girlfriend was stopped by the guards for cruising in the inside lane, so it seems not all the guards know either.

Customer: It's mad. They build these roads and then don't tell anyone how to use them!

Why men and women will always be at odds

16 April 2010

An Italian customer told me this gem one day . . .

Customer: You know why men and women will never understand each other?

Barber: Is this a joke, now, or a pearl of wisdom?

Customer: A joke? No, this is knowledge. This is so you can understand women better.

Barber: That's a big claim you're making, but go on, let's hear it.

Customer: Okay, it's real simple: women need to feel loved to have sex, and men need to have sex to feel loved.

Barber: Profound.

Mortgage increase!

17 April 2010

Customer: I can't believe the banks are putting the mortgage rates up. We bailed them out, and now they're sticking it to us. There will be more increases on the way.

Barber: The rates were supposed to stay the same until September. I wish they'd let us get off our knees before they hit us with this. I can imagine there'll be a lot more repossession now.

Customer: It's just not right. It was greed that got us into this mess—pure greed!

Barber: And you know what that means: the bankers had totally abandoned their discipline and threw away the rule book. How did that happen in ten years? Ask anyone who tried to get a mortgage or a loan in the eighties. There's even a story that the banks in America thought they'd eradicated risk and could loan to people with no income, no job and no assets. They were called 'ninja mortgages'! A customer told me there was an economist in the nineteenth century who thought the banking system would only work if it adhered to Christian principles. And guess what! Greed isn't one of them!

Limerick in a nutshell

18 April 2010

Customer: Limerick has no jobs, no minister and no bishop, but they have the pubs open on Good Friday!

The Icelandic volcano

19 April 2010

Sky News is on the shop television, and the story covering the Icelandic volcano is on . . .

Customer: What are the odds?

Barber: The odds on what?

Customer: We get the best weather we've had in years, and then, out of nowhere, for the first time in two hundred years, there's a huge volcano in Iceland, and the ash blocks out the sun!

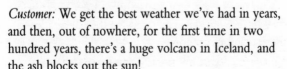

Pet hates

20 April 2010

Customer: I was in a nice restaurant the other day having my lunch when a woman came over to clear the table next to me. The tables are very close together, and when she took away the plates she came back with a spray and a cloth. Well, I couldn't believe what she did: she soaked the table with the spray, and it was like a mist in the air. I could smell it, and it was like fly-killer—really pungent. I was thinking, 'If I can smell it then this stuff is getting on my food.' It put me right off.

Barber: I had that happen to me too! It really is a bad idea. I cringe when I see the cleaning products coming out!

The ash cloud

21 April 2010

I've had almost every customer in the last few days tell me they know someone stuck in an airport somewhere in Europe. One customer had a friend stuck in Spain. 'Well, that's not such a bad place to be stuck,' I said. 'Well, you're wrong there,' he replied. 'It's been raining.'

There was black rain in Reykjavík because of the ash from the Eyjafjallajökull volcano, and one of the papers had a photo of the dust cloud and the headline 'Europe's 9/11!' The dust cloud had spread over most of Europe and had forced the planes to be grounded, as the dust plays havoc with jet engines and causes them to fail. It's a natural disaster of biblical proportions. But here's something I heard from the barber's chair while talking about the volcano:

Customer: Did you know that two hundred years ago there was a large volcano in Iceland and that it caused crops to fail all over Europe? Even as far away as North America the dust cloud was seen. Well, after the crops failed there was a shortage of food, and this food shortage caused the French to revolt in 1789.

Sometimes it snows in April!

22 April 2010

Customer: I can't believe it's snowing again—never saw anything like it: a blizzard of snow and then the sun comes out and it's warm again!

Barber: Tell me about it! I was up the mountains last week, and there was snow still—in patches, but up to a foot deep. It's nearly two months since the snow fell.

Customer: In the country there's a saying: 'If there's snow on the mountains it's waiting for more.'

The Choctaw Indians

26 April 2010

Customer: Have you heard of the Choctaw Indians?
Barber: No, I can't say I have. Why?
Customer: Well, I heard you talking about the Famine to that last customer, and I thought of a story I'd heard about the Choctaw Indians. The tribe was forced to move from their homeland around the Mississippi to Oklahoma to free up land for European settlers, and many died on the way. It became known as the Trail

of Tears. When the people heard about the Irish Famine they were reminded of the suffering they themselves had gone through, and they collected money among themselves to send to Ireland in 1847. They sent $710 to the Irish people—about a million or more in today's money—for famine relief. Quite an impressive sum!

Barber: That's some story!

Drink-and-drive holidays

24 April 2010

Customer: I had an idea to post on the web site for business ideas. It's called 'Your country, your call'. Have you heard of it?

Barber: Oh, yeah, I saw the ad on TV one night. What's your idea?

Customer: Drink-driving holidays! Imagine going away with the lads to a hotel, and you get cars to drive to the pub, where you can smoke inside and have a load of beer and then drive back to the hotel. The road would obviously have to be closed to other traffic, like a road specifically for the purpose, with rubber barriers on the sides for safety. Can you imagine the number of lads who'd love that? They'd come from all over Europe—stag parties and all. It's a winner.

Barber: I can't imagine them going for that!

Dodgy hair

25 April 2010

Customer: I hate my hair. It's so flat my friends call it Lego hair—you know, like the hair that Lego people have!

Barber: Brilliant!

Water is the new oil!

26 April 2010

Barber: I'd put money on Mr Ballygowan backing up that claim.

Customer: Well, it's true. There are people going round the country dowsing for water and analysing it. If it's good, and if there's a large amount of water, they buy the land!

Barber: So they expect the water from the reservoirs to get worse?

Customer: They're banking on it. It'll be hard to get decent water in the future unless you pay for it!

Orders from head office

27 April 2010

Our friend from the bookies pops his head in to tell the whole shop that there's going to be trouble over Máire Geoghegan-Quinn's pension if she doesn't refuse it. 'Trouble, I tell ye!' And off he went up the street, laughing out loud.

Customer: Is your man for real?

Barber: Ah, he does that all the time.

Customer: Mad as a box of frogs. He should be doing stand-up.

Barber (holding up a back mirror): How is that now?

Customer: Can you put a straight line across the back there?

Barber: Are you serious? We didn't do that the last time?

Customer: I know, but they're the orders from headquarters.

Barber: You mean the wife?

Customer: I do—she who must be obeyed.

Barber: Well, we better do it, then, or we'll both be in trouble . . . There, that's it now.

Customer: These are the things that make life easier as you get older. You see, if she's happy then I'm happy.

Barber: Now that's sound advice!

Identity crisis

28 April 2010

Customer (an older gent): I saw coverage of Irish people stuck in airports on the news, and I was taken aback by their attitude. This expectant arrogance is becoming the norm in society. They were demanding that the Government do something to get them home; they demanded that the airports get them to their destination! It's not the Irish way. Sadly, we're becoming a people the likes of which we'd once have despised.

Hello, sunshine

29 April 2010

Customer: The girls are all out looking well. Amazing what a little sun can do, eh?

Barber: I know. I bet there are cars crashing round Stephen's Green right now because the drivers are all rubbernecking!

Customer: Ah, the Green would be the place, all right.

Tough critics

1 May 2010

There were a few lads in the shop, and they were commenting on the women walking past the window . . . sunny day. . . short skirts. . .

Customer 1: Hey, lads, check out this bird. She'll be coming by in a second.

Customer 2: Jaysus, you must be joking. I wouldn't ride her into battle. She's bleedin' Dot Cotton!

Customer 1: Sure what would you know, the state of your bird!

Customer 2: My bird's got great legs and you know it.

Customer 1: I've seen better legs hanging out of a nest!

Going to the ball

2 May 2010

Customer (a young doctor): Just a tidy-up. I'm not due a haircut for another week or two, but I've a sex-trafficking ball to go to tonight.

Barber: Did you just say a sex-trafficking ball?

Customer: I just realised how that sounds. It's a ball to raise awareness and money to stop sex trafficking, that's all.

Barber: Well, it's an unfortunate title.

Customer: Not as bad as the rape ball we went to a few months ago! It was for the Rape Crisis Centre.

Tiger tramps

3 May 2010

During the good old days of the Celtic Tiger, a homeless person came into the shop one morning and approached me.

Homeless person: Hi, can I have some money to get a breakfast? I'm starving.

Barber (handing him a couple of euro): Okay.

Homeless person (looking at the coin in the palm of his hand, then back at me): Where am I supposed to get a breakfast for that?

Yes, that really happened!

An ecumenical matter

4 May 2010

Customer: A friend of mine was talking to a young parish priest about his son recently, asking him for advice on how to keep him out of trouble during the dreaded teenage years. So the priest says, 'Get the lad into sports. We always said it's sport or sex at that age, so get them busy with the sport and he'll be just fine.' 'Okay,' my friend says, 'that's good advice.' He's a bit of a chancer, you know, and he ended the conversation by asking the priest, putting on a cute-hoor accent, 'And what sport do you play yourself, father?' He said you'd want to see the look he got! Never answered the question, though!

Cromwell revisited

5 May 2010

Customer: You know the way St Patrick got rid of the snakes in Ireland and was canonised later on?

Barber: Sure we all know that.

Customer: Well, I wonder, in light of all that's happened with the church, you know, the abuse and scandals and all, if Cromwell will be regarded in a different light in a few hundred years by the historians. He tried to get rid of the priests in Ireland and used to burn down the churches during the Penal times.

Barber: I'm not so sure they'd see it that way!

Girls of summer

7 May 2010

Customer: I love this weather. When the girls are out looking summery it does you good.

Barber: If I had a euro for every time someone said that . . .

Customer: Just look at her—stunning! And to think I almost missed her going by! You should get wing-mirrors on the front of the shop so we could see them coming!

Skin cancer

8 May 2010

Lots of older customers have skin cancer on the top of their ears from sun exposure. It's a place you wouldn't normally think of putting sun block, but if you do it now you won't have a problem when you're older. Skin cancer is the most common type of cancer in Ireland, and it's no wonder, really, when after a sunny day most people are burned. I guess sunny days are so rare we forget to use sun block. I've done it myself.

The scalp is another area that needs protection if you have a very short haircut or a shaved head, so it's important to use sun block on a scalp covered with short or thinning hair. You can have a look at the Irish Cancer Society's site: www.cancer.ie/sunsmart.

Exam hairstyle

9 May 2010

Customer (with very long hair): Will you leave my hair long over my ears and over my collar at the back, please?

Barber: Okay. The weather is getting better, though. You'll be very warm with all that hair.

Customer: I know, but I've a lot of my study material recorded, and I put it on my iPod. So if you leave my hair long over my ears no-one will see the headphones, and if it's over my collar at the back I can run the wire from the headphones down into my shirt from the back.

Barber: You should get an A just for coming up with that!

'Cash for gold'
10 May 2010

Customer: There's been a spate of robberies since they started this 'cash for gold' promotion. Lads are breaking into houses to get gold to sell. They don't ask for receipts. I guess not many people would have receipts anyway.

Barber: There are people out there who'd take the gold out of your teeth.

Customer: It's just as well they bury them deep!

No more haystack hair in the morning
12 May 2010

In the morning does your hair look like a bird's nest, with bits sticking out everywhere? Well, I was cutting an older gent's hair the other day, and he shared a solution . . .

Customer: Why don't barbers use a hot towel to finish the hair any more?

Barber: What does that do?

Customer: Well, I used to live in London years ago, and they always finished my hair with a hot towel. I use it most days to get my hair to sit down in the mornings. You put a facecloth or towel into hot water—as hot as you can stand with your hands—then squeeze the excess water and put it on your head for a minute or two. It seems to steam-iron your hair flat onto your head.

Barber: Yes, it would do that. Brilliant—I'll be telling everyone about that.

Greece frightening

13 May 2010

Barber: This bail-out for Greece is frightening. €750 billion. Lenihan says we'll make a profit, as we're borrowing the funds at a cheaper rate than the one at which we're loaning it to the Greeks—but that's only if they pay us back!

Customer: If they don't we'll all be shovelling shite!

How much is a billion?

14 May 2010

Customer: Every year the figures in the papers for national debts are rapidly increasing. It was hundreds of millions; now it's hundreds of billions. But a billion in the US is different from a billion in the UK. A billion in England is a million million: that's 1 with twelve zeros; in the US it's a thousand million: that's 1 with nine zeros. I don't know if we use the American value or the English.

Barber: After a million I'm lost. I tried to enter a billion in the calculator on my phone, to divide it, and I could only enter ten million. There wasn't enough room for all the zeros!

Customer: Here's a good way to remember it: a million seconds is 12 days; a billion seconds is 31 years; and a trillion seconds is 31,688 years!

Ferry boom!

15 May 2010

Barber: Looks like the ferries will be doing okay for a while. People are saying they've changed for the better in the last few years, and it looks like the ash cloud will be disrupting flights for a while longer.

Customer: It's true, all right. The boats haven't been this busy since the Famine!

Random pub story

16 May 2010

Customer: In a pub in Dublin there were a few lads who'd always get phone calls at the bar from their wives telling them to come home. You'd mostly hear the lads say to the barman, 'Tell her I'm not here.' This happened one day in the pub, and, minutes later, in walks a woman with a dinner tray—knife and fork, the whole lot—and plonks it down on the table in front of her husband. She stares at him for a minute, and there isn't a sound in the pub or a word said between the two. She turns and walks back across the bar towards the door smiling, 'cause she's got him good and mortified in front of everyone. But just as she reaches the door her husband shouts out, 'You forgot the sauce!' Well, the whole place erupted with laughter! Never saw that woman again.

More jobs lost!

17 May 2010

Customer (a pensioner): What's going on with the Government. I mean, they're closing down businesses everywhere: there's Quinn Insurance, the head shops, and now they closed a load of brothels in town. All those girls will have to sign on the dole, you know!

Ladyboys in Zanzibar

18 May 2010

I miss the stories of excess and the surreal things that happened in Dublin back in the Celtic Tiger era. But this has to be my favourite. We had heard stories like this, as you would from people coming back from holidays abroad, but to hear about it happening in Dublin . . .

Customer (a student): We were all out last night in Zanzibar [a pub], and it was packed—full of girls—so the lads decided to stay, and we all got hammered. Some of us were up dancing, some of us were chatting up girls, but one of our mates had pulled a ladyboy.

Barber: Ladyboys? In Dublin?

Customer: Yeah, there's a few around—they're mostly Thai, I think. So we're trying to tell him, but he's having none of it. He thought we were winding him up. With the beer-goggles on he thought she was a babe, but we were sober enough to know she was a he.

Barber: So what did you do?

Customer: We went back over to get him, and at this stage he was getting off with the yoke, so we grabbed him and dragged him out of there! He still doesn't believe it was a ladyboy.

Barber: That was a lucky escape—it could've been *The Crying Game* all over again!

'Don't Feed the Gondolas'!

19 May 2010

We were talking about the television programme when a customer told us the story behind the name. In a meeting about doing up an area in Cork with the tourists in mind, the customer told us it was suggested that they get some gondolas for the river. The idea seemed to go down well in the room until someone said, 'It's all very well for you to suggest putting gondolas on the river, but who's going to feed them!'

Missing ducks

20 May 2010

Customer: I heard the ducks are disappearing down in the park since that new Chinese takeaway opened!

Barber: No such thing as coincidence!

The Muslim perspective

21 May 2010

Talking to a Muslim about Ramadan.

Customer: Well, I fast every day during Ramadan. From sunrise to sunset I don't eat or drink.

Barber: Can you have a drink of water?

Customer: No, nothing can pass my lips during the daylight!

Barber: How can you do that when you're working? It must be hard to do even if you don't work.

Customer: It is hard, but they're the rules.

Barber: I'm always amazed at how you follow the rules of your religion so exactly, even when the rules are so strict. Would you not have a drink if there was no-one around? Who would see?

Customer: Allah would see!

Sell your body!

22 May 2010

Talking to a medical student about the bodies they work on for research.

Customer: I was in the room on my own, and it was freezing, so I opened a window. It was quite warm outside, and it never even crossed my mind, but when the lecturer came in he went nuts. 'The cadavers have to be kept cold,' he says. 'They decompose rapidly!' Man, I felt so stupid. I didn't have the window open long, but if he hadn't come in when he did the cadaver would have been unusable.

Barber: Where do they get the bodies? I know they're donated, but how would you go about it. Do you sign up?

Customer: Ours come from abroad. That way, you don't end up working on your granddad! But yeah, you can sign up. They pay for it too, I think.

Barber: You have me thinking now: I wonder if they'd give an advance payment or a deposit!

Something's up underground

23 May 2010

Barber: There was an earthquake in west Clare last week!

Customer: I didn't hear about that. There must be

something going on underground with the earthquake in Clare and the volcano in Iceland!

Fish and chips

24 May 2010

We were talking about the fresh-cod scandal—the chippers using cheap fish—when a customer took us back to the heyday of Burdock's chip shop at Christ Church.

Customer: I remember queuing outside Burdock's after closing time on cold winter nights years ago. There would be a long queue outside, and there would be people from all walks of life: celebrities, politicians and all! People would wait as long as it took to get the chips, and once you were inside it was nice and warm. They had a coal-fired frier, and there was a lad who would keep shovelling the coal into the furnace in a corner, like a steam train. They used lard to fry the chips—big square blocks of it. I saw them putting a block in the frier one night when I was there. They really were the best chips you could get.

Barber: I remember it well. I used to keep them under my coat for the walk home when it was freezing out. They were too hot to eat. Probably the coal furnace made the oil hotter than the modern friers today.

Customer: It went up in flames, so the coal-burner had to go back in 1998, and I don't think it was ever the same after—but that's just me. Some people said it was a Maguire and Patterson job. But that's just rumour, I thought, till it went up again in 2009. Then I started to wonder!

Lumpy custard

25 May 2010

Customer: My son is six years old, and he was staying with his grandparents recently. As he's fond of custard, his granddad was making some for him. So when he served it, my son examined it and told him he didn't want it. 'Why?' his granddad asked. 'Is there something wrong with it?' 'Yes,' he said, 'there's no lumps in it!' His granddad explained that custard isn't supposed to have lumps in it. And my son told him, 'But my Mam always makes it with lumps!'

Brussels sprouts

26 May 2010

Customer: I've been trying to get my kids to eat better food lately: more greens and fruit. It's not easy, though.

Barber: I know. You probably know the one about pretending a piece of broccoli is a miniature tree.

Customer: I do. I've also been telling them Brussels sprouts are Cabbage McNuggets!

Eurovision

27 May 2010

Barber: There's a lot of talk about the Irish entry for the Eurovision. Did you hear it?

Customer: No, not yet. They say she has a chance, though. The song is meant to be good this time.

Barber: If we win, how could we possibly afford to stage the Eurovision now that we're looking for pennies just to keep the lights on?

Customer: RTE will have to send out a sniper if we get through to the final!

Gardening tip
28 May 2010

Barber: I've been trying to get the weeds out of the garden, and I tried that stuff that kills the weeds and turns them black, but it didn't work very well.

Customer: That stuff is rubbish. Use diesel.

Barber: Diesel?

Customer: Yeah, diesel. It kills everything. You have to reseed it after no more weeds, though. Doesn't smell great for a week or two, but, hey—it works!

Highlights
29 May 2010

Customer: I want to get highlights in my hair.

Barber: Okay, that would look well. Do you want them very light blonde?

Customer: I don't mind as long as they aren't car-thief yellow.

So true!
30 May 2010

A customer was telling a story about a crazy night out on the town that ended with some of the lads in the garda station and one in the hospital. When he left another customer said:

Customer: You must hear all sorts in here.

Barber: We do indeed.

Customer: I've read thrillers that didn't have that much action in them!

Not so healthy!

31 May 2010

Customer (from the Netherlands): Why is it that your Minister for Health is obese?

Everyone burst out laughing.

The HSE

1 June 2010

Customer (young student): I was doing work experience in the HSE, and, man, I can't get over the waste in there.

Barber: I've had customers tell me about it. No-one seems to do a lot.

Customer: It's like that, all right. I spent days surfing the web, and no-one said anything. One day they had a meeting, and there were ten people at it. They ordered thirty sandwiches at four euro a pop—for ten people! I asked why they ordered so much and was told they got a selection, 'cause not everyone likes the same. So why don't they just ask what people want before they order! It's nuts! So then they asked me to stay on when I finish work experience.

Barber: Are you going to?

Customer: No, I told them I'd like to work for a living!

Overqualified!

2 June 2010

Customer: My daughter is a lawyer, and she was working in town a few weeks ago. She had to stay in for lunch, so she ordered a pizza with some friends. When it arrived she saw that the lad who delivered it had passed the bar with her. Now he's delivering pizza!

Barber: We could all be delivering pizza soon, the way things are going.

Barber-shop phone calls

3 June 2010

The phone rang. I answered it, and as soon as I had said, 'Hello. You're through to the barber shop,' the caller hung up. I went back to the customer whose hair I was cutting and told him what had happened . . .

Barber: That's the fourth time today: people keep ringing and hanging up. It happens all the time!

Customer: I do that myself to see if you're open.

Barber: What! Why don't you say anything?

Customer: Well, I'd feel pretty stupid saying, 'Hello, are you open?' So I just hang up and come down!

Barber: The mystery is solved!

Do you drink much, Mr Murphy?

4 June 2010

A customer told me his granddad, Mr Murphy, wasn't well, and the doctor was called. After examining the patient, the doctor asked a few questions . . .

'So,' the doctor says, 'talk me through a normal day

from the time you get up in the morning.'

My granddad tells him he gets up and has breakfast. Then he says, 'I ramble down to the pub for one or two and pick up a paper.'

'What do you do after that?' asks the doctor.

'I'd go home for something to eat, then, around lunchtime.'

'Very good,' says the doctor. 'And then after lunch what would you do?'

'Well, I'd ramble down to the pub for one or two, you know—watch the horses on the telly.'

'Well, when someone says one or two drinks it tends to be more. Anyway, what do you do then?'

'Ah, I'd stay there till my tea was ready, and I'd go home.'

'And then after tea what would you do?'

'If there's nothing on the telly I'd ramble down to the pub for one or two and a bit of a chat. You know yourself.'

'And is that what you would do most days?'

'Yeah, most days.'

'Well, I have news for you, Mr Murphy: you're an alcoholic!'

'Alcoholic? Ah, no,' he says, almost laughing. 'Sure I just ramble down for one or two!'

Exam beards

5 June 2010

There's a new style this year among the students that's becoming known as the 'exam beard'! They're so focused on their studies that shaving isn't a priority. Some of the students coming in look like they should be off to Woodstock: long hair and beards! Maybe the tie-dye T-shirts will reappear too!

Cracking weather!
7 June 2010

Barber: The weather is bang on time again—every year when everyone is studying for exams.

Customer: It's great. You know, I think the Donegal postman is right with his predictions.

Barber: I heard he watches the mountains and the birds and can tell the weather from that—mostly the birds, I'd say. I can tell when the weather is getting better because their skirts get shorter!

Drop-dead gorgeous
8 June 2010

Barber: I remember a barber who was finishing up a cut and had picked up the back mirror to show his customer the back of his hair in the mirror. But the customer was asleep, so he tapped him a couple of times on the shoulder, and didn't your man slump forward onto the basin! Dead!

Customer: Dead? Jesus, how did that happen?

Barber: Must have been a heart attack, they said. The barber cutting his hair never noticed.

Customer: Did he take the money for the haircut out of the dead lad's wallet?

Barber: Sure he did, and the dead lad must've liked the haircut, because he told me he got a decent tip too!

Criminal makeovers!

9 June 2010

Something came up in the shop today that started a
conversation about crime and criminals. I remembered
a few lads from a barber shop in town who we'd bump
into on nights out and who were well known for
doing makeovers on lads who were wanted by the
guards. They'd shave their hair off, or their beards, or
colour the hair to totally change the appearance of
Dublin's most wanted. But, anyway, it led to the telling
of this story:

Barber: Years ago in a shop I worked in in town we
were all busy cutting away when a guy burst into the
shop a little out of breath and looking a bit nervous,
but he sat down quietly, and everyone went back to
cutting and talking. So a couple of minutes later one of
the other barbers finished the haircut he was doing,
and this particular guy was next. He got into the chair
and said he wanted his head shaved close. 'No
problem,' the other barber said and began cutting.

Now, in the meantime, from where I worked I
could see up the street, and there was a bit of
excitement: some guards had arrived. It all seemed to
be happening outside the newsagent's. Then the guards
began walking down towards the barber shop with the
owner of the newsagent. The lad having his hair
shaved had just realised this, and he tore his gown off,
ran out the door of the shop and down the street as fast
as he could, with the guards starting after him.

The owner of the newsagent, who we knew well,
stopped outside our door and told us the lad had
robbed the shop; but someone saw him ducking into

our shop, so the guards were walking down to nab him when he bolted. 'I hope they catch him,' said the newsagent. 'Well,' the other barber said, 'they won't have any trouble spotting him: he ran off with half his hair cut!'

Driving lessons

10 June 2010

Customer: I have to tell you this one. I'm a driving instructor, and I took a woman out today to do a lesson. Sitting in the car, she puts on her seatbelt, starts the engine clutch in, puts the car in gear and lets off the handbrake, indicates to move out onto the road, but she never looks! So I say to her, 'Have a look in the mirror.' And she looks, shocked. Instead of looking behind in the rear-view mirror she leans forward and starts examining her face and says, 'Oh, God, is it a spot?'

Barber: You're scaring me now!

The Blackwater men

11 June 2010

Customer: Have you been down to Blackwater recently?

Barber: No, the weather hasn't been great for the last few summers, so I haven't been down.

Customer: Did you ever hear about the Blackwater men when you were down there?

Barber: No, what's that all about?

Customer: Well, it's a story seldom told, but around the

coast there are hundreds of shipwrecks, because there's a bank near Blackwater, and the lads down there would put a lantern on a donkey and lead it along the headland at night when there was a ship in the distance. The ship's captain would see the light and follow it, thinking it was following another ship through a safe course, and they'd find themselves beached on the Blackwater bank. The captain and crew would go ashore to get help to tow the ship off the bank, and most of the time when they returned the ship would be stripped of its cargo. There's a church in Ballygarrett, near Curracloe, where they say the pews are made from wood stolen from a ship called the *Irrawaddy*. It ran aground on the bank in 1856.

When time slows down

14 June 2010

Barber: It's a really slow day today. I can't believe it's only half two!

Customer: I know those days—feels like it'll never end. Do you know what you call that?

Barber: No.

Customer: Groundhog Day!

Stag parties

15 June 2010

Customer: I'm going on a stag weekend, but it's not abroad—it's in Galway.

Barber: That's the recession for you!

Customer: Yeah, not many going abroad for weekends

any more. It was a bit mental for a while there. If you had a few friends getting married in the same year it was expensive. You know, I'd rather get a summons in the post than another wedding invitation. Anyway, I was on holiday in Poland last year, and we went to Auschwitz, and a girl there, who was like a tour guide, asked us where we were from. 'Ireland,' we said. 'Oh,' she says, 'usually the Irish who come here are on stag parties and smell of alcohol!'

Barber: Not exactly an ideal place for a stag!

Customer: When you ask people who've been to Auschwitz what it's like they say, 'Oh, it's amazing. You should go!' Do people know it was a death camp? I wonder sometimes.

Traffic warden

16 June 2010

The local traffic warden used to get his hair cut in the shop, and one day when he came in the shop was quiet, but it began to get busier as I was cutting his hair. When I finished his hair I took his gown off, and everyone could see his uniform, but it wasn't until he stood up and put on his hat that almost all the customers evacuated the shop, each one saying, 'I'll be back in a minute—just putting some money in the meter!'

A new man

17 June 2010

Barber (putting the finishing touches to a haircut): Now, how's that?

Customer: That's some transformation: my own dog won't know me!

No more speeding tickets!

18 June 2010

Barber: I got caught recently coming off the M50. I couldn't believe it. I was slowing down, and there they were, hiding behind a bus shelter! They got me.

Customer (a guard): Well, there's a way you can never get a ticket again, you know.

Barber: So tell me what it is!

I could see the lads waiting on the couch behind me sitting up to hear what the guard was going to say next.

Customer: Don't drive over the speed limit!

Dangerous muesli

19 June 2010

Customer: A friend of mine drowned in his muesli the other day!

Barber: What?

Customer: Yeah, he was dragged under by a strong currant!

Hard of hearing

20 June 2010

I was about to begin cutting an elderly customer's hair, and I asked him what he thought of the present Fine Gael crisis, as Enda Kenny had just fired Richard Bruton. 'Hold on a minute there. I have to take out the hearing aid.' He takes it out and puts it away. 'Now,' he says, 'you can talk to yourself!'

Going grey

21 June 2010

Customer: I'm really going grey—just look at that [holding up the trimmings that have fallen onto the gown].

Barber: Well, at least you have a thick head of hair. I wouldn't mind what colour it is as long as I have hair!

Customer: Can you just cut the grey ones and leave the rest?

Viva Las Vegas

22 June 2010

Barber: Hey, how did you get on in Vegas?

Customer: I won, believe it or not. I won the Poker Classic!

Barber: That's brilliant. Well done!

Customer: Well, I got out of there with a small fortune, but I got an invitation to go back to Vegas, all expenses paid, flights and a penthouse—the whole lot—so I thought, 'That's great. I'm off on a free trip!' But in a week they cleaned me out. Very clever, though, inviting me back and then fleecing me! So I didn't feel like a winner for long.

Elvis lives

23 June 2010

There was a character who regularly came into the shop dressed as Elvis—the Vegas Elvis. He was about mid-forties, with black hair in the Vegas style and big sideburns. He spoke like Elvis too. He seemed to be fond of a pint or four. Anyway, he used to sell poems that he said Elvis told him to write: channeled writing from the other side. They were about his daughter, Lisa Marie, and stuff about him not being happy about the way he died. So, one busy Saturday, Elvis came in for a trim. The shop was packed, and he'd been drinking. He was a quiet drunk and just sat down and waited his turn, until an Elvis song came on the radio, and he was up like a man possessed, doing all the Presley poses and pulling the moves and singing along. It was hilarious. He wasn't at all phased by everyone laughing. Then, when the song ended, he sat back down quietly as if nothing had happened!

The older generation

26 June 2010

Customer: What was that you were just doing to that young lad's hair?

Barber: He was getting highlights.

Customer: Highlights? Sure that's for women.

Barber: Well, the latest thing for the men is the GHD.

Customer: The GHD? What's that?

Barber: It straightens the hair like an iron, but for your hair. Women used to use an iron on a paper bag to straighten their hair in the sixties.

Customer: And, tell me, do they wear their sister's knickers too?

Vuvuzelas
27 June 2010

Customer: Man, I can't stand the noise from those vuvuzelas. It's driving me mad watching the matches.

Barber: I'm getting used to it at this stage.

Customer (in the waiting area): They're not so bad, lads. I'll tell you what's worse: being in Croke Park with a bad hangover and a kid behind you with an air horn!

People aged rapidly in old Ireland
28 June 2010

Customer: I was doing some research on my family, and I found discrepancies in the ages on a census. After looking into it, it turned out that the old-age pension was introduced here on 1 January 1909, and people lied about their age on the census so they'd qualify for the pension earlier!

Barber: So it's not a new thing, then. I remember, in the eighties, recession people with jobs dressing down to go and collect their dole money—must be something in the genes.

The Vegas look

8 July 2010

Customer: Get rid of the lamb chops there. I look like Elvis in Vegas!

The wordy customer

10 July 2010

Customer: I don't mean to be permutatious, but could you take a little more off the fringe there?

Barber: Now there's a word!

Traveller tricks

11 July 2010

Customer (a Traveller, arriving in a very busy barber shop on a Saturday morning): Lads, do you mind if I skip the queue? I have to be at a funeral in Wexford in an hour and a half!

Barber: Does anyone mind if Blackie here skips the queue?

Customer (the Traveller): I just need to get the back cleaned up. It'll only take a minute!

Barber: Okay. No objections? Take a seat there. You're lucky they let you skip ahead—there's been fights over less!

Customer: That's great. Thanks, lads. Only I have to be at the funeral, you know . . . Just a little off the back there.

Barber: Now then, how's that?

Customer: Does it look okay now? Maybe you better take a little off the sides to match it up.

Barber: Okay—just a little, though. Now, how's that?

Customer: The top looks too long now you've done the sides, do you think?

Barber: Only this once, and seeing you're going to a funeral, I'll do it.

Customer: That's it now—lovely. How much?

Barber: It's fourteen euro, please.

Customer: Fourteen euro? Sure I only wanted the back tidied up!

Barber: But I gave you a full haircut!

Customer: Here [handing me a fistful of loose change], that's all I have. I have to go—have to get to that wedding in an hour and a half!

Spain wins the World Cup

12 July 2010

Customer: That was a terrible match to watch! Fourteen yellow cards and one red. The Dutch play dirty. Did you have a bet on?

Barber: No, my money was on the octopus!

Time for a trim

13 July 2010

Barber: You normally work on a Tuesday. Are you off today?

Customer: No, I'm working, but I slipped out to get my hair cut. It grows on their time, so I get it cut on their time!

Oxegen

17 July 2010

Customer: I'm just back from Oxegen. I'm *so* tired.

Barber: How was it down there? The weather was terrible—again!

Customer: It rained on the Saturday, so we were soaked through, and then later it started to get cold, so when we got back to the campsite it was miserable. We were all cold, tired and hungry, so we just started forcing the cans down. I remember sitting there feeling miserable and wishing I was at home tucked up in bed. We didn't even take off our shoes, which were covered in muck, when we got into the sleeping bags. Then we woke up roasted: the sun had come out, and we all felt shit. Mucky, sweaty, and it was early, so we just started knocking back the cans again. The bands made it all worth while, though. They were great. Jay-Z was brilliant, and Eminem.

Barber: That sounds hellish to me. Was there any tent-burning this year?

Customer: No, there was lots of security.

Barber: Last year Kings of Leon were there, and that song 'Sex on Fire' was in the charts, and people in the campsite were singing, 'Your tent is on fire.'

Women

19 July 2010

Customer: Women: can't live with them, can't live without them—and sheep can't do the washing up!

Recession stress

20 July 2010

Customer: There are two types of people in this recession: the ones who buckle under the pressure of their debts or can't go back to a simpler life, and the ones who just say, 'Fuck it!'

Barber: If you owe less than lads like Seánie Fitzpatrick then you've no need to worry. If they're not feeling the pressure then no-one should be.

Country crossroads

21 July 2010

We were talking about unusual car crashes.

Customer: Down the country where I live there's a crossroads in the middle of nowhere. The road has no lighting at night, and there are no traffic lights. A few years ago a car was coming up to the crossroads, and it kept going, never dropping its speed. Then, out of nowhere, another car hit him head on, just at the edge of the crossroads. Neither driver saw the other coming. The guards turned up, and luckily the two lads who crashed were okay. The crash was a mystery for ages until I heard from one of the drivers that he always turned off his lights coming up to the junction and that he could see if someone else was coming easily, because the oncoming car's headlights would be obvious in the pitch dark. That night it turned out that both drivers had turned off their lights approaching the crossroads and ploughed straight into each other!

Camping

22 July 2010

Barber: Camping is huge this year. People are not really talking about it, but the campsites are busy!

Customer: I went camping myself. The place was really busy on the bank holiday, but it's even more basic than I thought. The first morning I woke up and headed off to get coffee and croissants, but there was nothing available. All the campers had everything with them. I thought there would be a shop or a café or something. It really is hardcore. You need to bring a serious amount of stuff with you.

Barber: No-frills holidays!

Miracle Grow

23 July 2010

Customer: My hair is growing like the grass lately! You must be putting something in the water: Miracle Grow or something!

Barber: Since the recession began, barbers have been dumping bags of keratin in the reservoirs.

Customer: What does keratin do?

Barber: It makes your hair and nails grow faster!

Customer: The way my hair is growing, you know I'd almost believe that.

Barber: Times like these, it's every man for himself. Would you like to buy a nail-clippers?

Baldness cure!

24 July 2010

Customer: Did you ever come across a cure for baldness that worked?

Barber: Yes, I found a great recipe online that's easy to make: it's just chopped onions, cayenne pepper and ginger, all soaked in alcohol for a few days. Then you strain it and rub the liquid into your scalp.

Customer (sits up in the chair, eyes wide open): Really?

Barber: No, I'm only pulling your leg!

The wonder of Oz

26 July 2010

Customer: Cut it shorter than usual. I'm off to Australia later today.

Barber: Are you going for long?

Customer: A year at least—seems to be jobs available again over there.

Barber: You're the third customer this morning who's heading off for work. It's amazing how many Irish people go to Australia. Most people have either been to Australia or they're going to Australia, and I never met anyone who didn't like it!

The cause of the boom

27 July 2010

Customer: I read lately about how the boom started. I was always wondering where all the money came from and how it just stopped as though someone flicked a switch.

Barber: So how did it start?

Customer: A huge amount of industry went to China because they were able to manufacture goods at a fraction of the cost. There was even a rumour that the Irish football jerseys were being made over there, but that's just hearsay. So, in a nutshell, they made a fortune, and workers, as you know, are paid a pittance. So China loaned this money to the American banks, and they had so much money coming in they were giving it away. Economies boomed, and people were overstretched, living on credit and getting big mortgages. Then China stopped the supply, and—bang!—the whole system fell apart!

Barber: So Bertie took the credit for the wave, when all he did was surf on it!

Jedward

28 July 2010

Customer: Don't even get me started on those two! It's music for the Teletubby generation!

Barber: Music? They couldn't carry a tune in a bucket!

Southill, Limerick

29 July 2010

Customer: A friend of mine went into a shop in Limerick, and he'd left his car parked outside for a few minutes. When he came back out it was gone. He ran over to the garda station, and, as it had just been taken, the guards jumped into a car and, with my friend, headed towards Southill. Within minutes they were out of the city, and, as they drove by a field, they stopped. One of the guards noticed the gate was open. They parked the car and walked back to the field, and there was the car. But there was no-one around, so the guards say to him, 'Stay down and be quiet,' and they all sat tight and waited. It wasn't long before they heard the lads who'd taken the car coming back, talking and laughing. When they got up close to the car the guards grabbed them and took them off. It turns out the lads had gone off somewhere to get drums of petrol, which they had with them when they were caught, to set the car on fire. They were obviously new to stealing cars!

In the army

30 July 2010

Barber: Were you away, or did you get that tan here?

Customer: Yeah, I was away. I'm in the Army Reserve, and we went to Lourdes a few weeks ago.

Barber: What was the army doing in Lourdes?

Customer: There's an international military pilgrimage to Lourdes every year.

Barber: I'm finding this hard to comprehend: you're telling me there's a military pilgrimage to Lourdes? How can that be possible! It sounds all wrong.

Customer: French soldiers used to go there in the forties to pray. It caught on, and more and more countries began to go. Now armies come from all over the world.

Barber: I see. And what do the soldiers pray for?

Customer: Mostly peace, I suppose!

Barber: Well, I've heard it all now!

Quick thinking

31 July 2010

A customer told me that he'd been in a car crash on the way home from a pub after having a few drinks. This was a good few years ago, before the drink-and-drive clampdown. He'd taken a corner at speed, lost control and scraped the car along a wall sideways, then came to a sudden stop when he hit a parked car. Uninjured, he got out and saw a pub across the road.

He went in and ordered two straight whiskeys and asked the barman for a receipt, which he put in his pocket. Then, after knocking back one, he emptied the second into a plant pot at the side of the bar but pretended to knock back the whiskey. He went back outside, and the guards had arrived.

He went over and told them that it was his car and that he'd lost control coming around the corner. The guards noticed the smell of alcohol on his breath and asked him if he'd been drinking, to which he replied, 'God, no! But I went into the bar over there to get a stiff drink to steady my nerves. Here,' he said. 'I think I still have the receipt in my pocket!'

The empathic barber

1 August 2010

Barber: Doing anything for the weekend? Will you have a few pints?

Customer: No, I have ME, so I'm very tired most of the time.

Barber: So what's that then?

Customer: It's an illness I've had for—

Barber: Jaysus, it's not contagious is it?

Customer: No, not at all, it's just that when I get a good night's sleep, instead of waking up refreshed I wake up feeling exhausted, every day. Some days are worse than others, though. I can't drink alcohol: it'd wipe me out for days. So I only have a few hours a day when I've enough energy to get out and about and get things done. I spend a lot of time just sitting around at home.

Barber: So you have a lot of time to yourself then, says you. That's lovely, isn't it?

A triumph
2 August 2010

Customer: On a bike-run at the weekend there was a guy with a vintage Triumph. It was in great condition, so I said to him I'd never seen one so good and with no oil leaks! To which he replied, 'Well, it would if it got any!'

Cover-up
3 August 2010

Customer: A lad I used to work with had three wigs of different lengths, and he'd go through them all, pretending his hair was getting longer, and when he wore the longest one for a while he'd announce he was off to the barbers to get it cut. He'd arrive back wearing the shortest one! He thought he was fooling everyone, but we all knew!

170

Nice job

4 August 2010

Customer: I'm a transparent-wall maintenance engineer.
Barber: What's that?
Customer: I clean the windows at the airport.

Shamrock Rovers v. Juventus

5 August 2010

Customer: Looking forward to the game tonight.
Juventus aren't playing in their home ground because
U2 are playing there tomorrow!
Barber: Sounds like it was a plan.
Customer: The Irish invasion!

Beauty salons

6 August 2010

Barber: There are so many beauty salons closing down
in the last year. They've been hit so hard in the
recession.
Customer: But Irish women don't look any less
beautiful than before.
Barber: So what are you saying? They were wasting
their money?

Bono's back

7 August 2010

Customer: What did Bono do to his back? He must
have slept on a cheap bed or something.
Barber: Well, he does do those high kicks on stage.

Customer: If you ask me, that pain in his back was all in his head!

Pass-remarkable
9 August 2010

Customer: I was out walking the pier in Dún Laoghaire with my girlfriend, and the weather was great, so we asked a lad to take a picture of us, and he spent a while looking at the screen, getting the picture in focus. He took the photo and handed me back the camera, and, as my girlfriend was walking off, he quietly says to me, with a big grin on his face, 'Your bird has a great rack!'

Barber: No wonder he spent a while focusing the camera: he was checking her out!

Soccer in the US
10 August 2010

Customer: Soccer will never take off in America. It's just not going to happen!

Barber: I heard a quote in a film: 'Americans will never embrace soccer!'

Customer: Who said that?

Barber: Homer Simpson in *The Simpsons Movie*!

Recession haircuts
11 August 2010

Customer: I see a lot of people are getting the recession haircut.

Barber: You mean a shaved head? But that's been around a long time.

Customer: It's really big in the States now. Lots of athletes and football players are wearing it.

Barber: Well, I can't imagine any football players feeling the pinch over there—it's just a fashion thing!

Some neck

12 August 2010

Woman barber (approaching a customer in the waiting area): You know the way you always give me a fiver tip?

Customer (a little surprised): Yeah . . .

Woman barber: Well, would there be any chance I could get an advance? It's just one of the girls is going out for our sandwiches, and I've no money!

More soccer in the US

13 August 2010

Customer: I was working in a bar in the States when the World Cup was on, and the Americans just don't get soccer. I had the TV on to see the games at work, and some of the lads at the bar watched it too.

Barber: What did they think of it?

Customer: The game ended in a draw, and they kept asking me who won. 'It's a draw,' I said, but they kept asking, 'But who won?'

Barber: They don't have games that end in a draw over there, as far as I know. They might have to change some of the rules to get it to the next level over there.

Customer: That's what I'm afraid of!

Best weather in years

16 August 2010

Customer: The Donegal postman was right! The weather here is just as he said it would be.

Barber: It's really good today. There's no-one around—must've all gone to the beach!

Customer: You should close the shop and head out there yourself with a mirror and a chair—make yourself a fortune!

First Irish toll road

17 August 2010

Customer: Do you know when the first toll road opened in Ireland?

Barber: Must be the one on the M50. That's the oldest I remember.

Customer: No, the first toll road here was the Carlow–Kilkenny road back in 1731!

Moving south

18 August 2010

Customer (a Protestant originally from the North): I moved down to Dublin in the late sixties, and back at home all my friends and neighbours were shocked.

Barber: Why were they shocked?

Customer: It was the biased perspective they had of life in the South. They really were horrified by the idea of me moving into a Catholic area. They were saying things like 'Those Catholics throw their rubbish out in the front garden—babies' nappies and all.' Terrible things. It turns out they'd heard all this but had never been down South to know what the reality was. So when I'd go back up to visit they were amazed to hear that it was nothing like that. I thought it was really funny. It still makes me laugh!

Barber: I imagine it's the same on both sides: stories played a part in keeping up the barriers. They demonised each other.

No point

19 August 2010

Barber: Will I trim your eyebrows? They're quite long.

Customer: Sure why would you do that—they'll only grow back again!

Some people

20 August 2010

Customer: I'm glad the Celtic Tiger is dead. I didn't like a lot of what was happening to people and their attitudes.

Barber: It did get out of hand, all right, but then we were new to all that: kids in the sweet-shop.

Customer: Well, that's a very diplomatic way of explaining it. I remember sitting outside a coffee shop, relaxing in town, having a cigarette, and a well-dressed woman walked by with a child, and she pointed to me as she went by, never catching my eye, like I wasn't there. She says to the child, 'Look at that dirty man smoking a cigarette. That's disgusting!' I couldn't believe my ears!

Barber: That's incredible!

Holidays in Ireland

21 August 2010

Customer: Great value in hotels here at the moment—must be all these ghost hotels that NAMA are running.

Barber: It used to be a different story: high prices and terrible service, in some places.

Customer: I remember staying in a big hotel years ago in the west. It was packed the week we were there. I'll always remember the breakfast we were served. It was disgusting: the fried eggs were like rubber. I was saying to the wife that I'd try the scrambled egg instead, and the lad at the next table overheard me and says, 'Don't get the scrambled egg—it's worse!' I ended up paying a fortune, and the kids were an extra eighty or hundred euro each a night. My son was four—sure he'd hardly wear the carpet!

A bad kebab

23 August 2010

Customer: I was so sick at the weekend. I was out on Saturday, and we were out all night drinking cocktails and shorts, and I was feeling fine—well hammered, though. And then I made a big mistake: I got a kebab on the way home—never felt so ill. I was on the couch all day yesterday, and I rang in sick today! Must have been food poisoning.

Barber: You were drinking shorts and cocktails all night, but it was the kebab on the way home that made you sick?

Long-distance swimmer

24 August 2010

Customer: A friend of mine swims every day. Regardless of the weather, he's out in the sea. He swims off the coast of Waterford, down at Helvick Head, and he was telling me recently he was swimming back to the harbour when he saw two American tourists. They get a lot of them down there—it's a beautiful spot. So he gets back to the harbour wall, just below the Yanks who were watching him, and he shouts out, 'Is this Wales?' To which they reply, 'No, this is Ireland.' 'Oh, no,' he says. 'I must have missed it!' And he kicks off the harbour and swims back out to sea, with the Americans standing there amazed!

Highlighted hair in schools

25 August 2010

Barber: All the lads are in getting their highlights cut out because they're going back to school. I always wonder why they're so hard on kids who have colour in their hair.

Customer (a teacher): Well, I can tell you why. I'd have agreed with you fifteen years ago when I argued the same issue with a principal in the school I was working in. It was mostly girls who had highlights then. So I won my case, and the kids were all getting highlights, and we let it go. Then, one day, a girl came into school with bright orange hair. We had to draw the line, and she was suspended. I asked her why she had done it, and she said she wanted to be different.

Barber: So by removing the ban you forced the rebels to the next level.

Customer: That's exactly it!

Faith

26 August 2010

Barber (during a conversation about faith): It's well known when there's an imminent threat to life that people turn to a higher power for help. Like a plane crash, for instance—most people will turn to prayer out loud, even.

Customer: Not always the case, though. When I was young I was with my parents, driving through the North of Ireland on a quiet country road late at night. There were lots of trees, I remember, so we were well into the country when we turned a corner, and there were about five men in balaclavas with guns or rifles—I can't remember exactly—but we thought that was it, with our Southern-reg. plates! We had no choice but to stop, and my dad rolled down the window when one of the guys came over to the driver's window. 'Are you Protestant or Catholic?' he asked. After a few seconds my dad says, 'Neither—we're atheists.'

Barber: But still, I bet he was praying it would work!

Customer: I know *I* was. It worked, all right. We made it through—scary moment, though!

Sunshine and rain

27 August 2010

Barber: The sun is back out. It was raining just a minute ago!

Customer (a student): I love this weather!

Barber: Are you serious?

Customer: Yeah, the girls see it's warm and sunny, and they come out in T-shirts, and then, when they're out walking around town, it rains, and it's like a wet T-shirt competition out there!

Barber: There's always an upside to everything if you look hard enough!

Shopping

28 August 2010

Barber: Are you doing anything for the weekend?

Customer: Yeah, I'm going to a party tonight with my girlfriend. We were in town all morning because she wanted to buy a dress, and she saw one in the first shop we went into but didn't get it, and she went off on a mad one, going to every shop in town, dragging me with her. Three hours later she decides to go back and get the dress she saw in the first shop!

Sex crime

29 August 2010

Customer: There was nothing in the papers or the radio but talk of whether to name or disclose the addresses of anyone convicted of sex crimes. It's an important issue, but it's like when a big story breaks there's nothing else discussed.

Barber: There was a story a customer told me about a woman in south Wales a few years ago who had her house vandalised by an anti-paedophile mob. They sprayed 'paedo' across her front door. It turned out when the police looked into it that she was a paediatrician. Information can be a dangerous thing in the wrong hands!

Customer: Maybe they were dyslexic!

The health service

30 August 2010

Customer: There's a Romanian woman who sells the *Big Issue* outside the shop I work in, and she's very friendly, so over the last year we've gotten to know her. But a while ago she disappeared for weeks, and no-one knew where she was. She had told us her husband wasn't well and they were waiting for an operation for him, and we started to think the worst. Then, out of the blue, last week she was back selling outside the shop again. We asked her where she'd been, and she told us that they'd been waiting for so long for her husband's operation that she decided to book flights home for herself and her husband. They went to the hospital, arranged the operation in Romania for free, had a holiday, saw the family and came back!

Barber: That's incredible. They could get the operation so quickly over there, and for free! What's going on over here?

Cuckoo land

31 August 2010

Customer: The sentences the judges are passing down for serious crimes are ridiculous. The law is no deterrent any more!

Barber: They're all living in cuckoo land, far removed from the real world. So are a lot of the politicians. Look at Pádraig Flynn's argument on 'The Late Late Show', for example, telling the nation that he was stretched by the cost of running his three houses, the maids and the cars. It would all be so funny if it wasn't so serious.